RAYMOND WEIL

Ingersoll
SINCE 1892

GUCCI
timepieces

PAIN

LONGINES

TISSOT

PIAGET

JAEGER-LECOULTRE

AP
AUDEMARS PIGUET

Chopard

TIMEX®

SEIKO

YSL

UMET

ORIS

ROLEX

MOVADO

IWC
International Watch Co Ltd, Schaffhausen, Switzerland

BVLGARI

RADO

FORTIS
swiss watches

gērald genta

Wristwatches

A CONNOISSEUR'S GUIDE

GUCCI

Wristwatches

A CONNOISSEUR'S GUIDE

FRANK EDWARDS

A FIREFLY BOOK

First published in Canada in 1997 by
Firefly Books Ltd.
3680 Victoria Park Avenue
Willowdale, Ontario M2H 3KI

Published in the U.S. by
Firefly Books (U.S.) Inc.
P.O. Box 1338, Ellicott Station
Buffalo, New York 14205

Cataloguing in Publication Data

Edwards, Frank
Wristwatches
a connoisseurs's guide
Includes Index
ISBN 1-55209-083-3
1. Wristwatches – History. I. Title.
TS 542.E38 1997 681. 1'14 C96-932061-2

This book was designed and produced by
Quintet Publishing Limited
6 Blundell Street, London N7 9BH

Creative Director: Richard Dewing
Art Director: Silke Braun
Designer: Ian Hunt
Senior Project Editor: Laura Sandelson
Editor: Maggie McCormick
Photographer: David Armstrong

Typeset in Great Britain by
Central Southern Typesetters, Eastbourne
Manufactured in Singapore by Eray Scan Pte Ltd
Printed in Singapore by Star Standard Industries (Pte) Ltd

PICTURE CREDITS

Abbreviations: *b* = bottom; *l* = left; *r* = right; *t* = top.

The Beyer Museum: p18*t*. Chronoswiss Uhren GmbH: p61*tl*. Andrew Ward, Life File: pp8*bl*, 18. The Mansell Collection: pp8*tr*, 9*tl*, 11. Thos. Mercer: p17*tr*. Patek Philippe archive: pp13*bl*, 23. Rolex archive: p127*tl*.

CONTENTS

The Publishers would like to thank the David Morris International Watch Room at Selfridges, Oxford Street, Harvey Nichols, Knightsbridge and 180 Bond Street, London, for their help in the compilation of this book.

Foreword

The Directory which follows contains the names of some 50 prestigious watch brands. What makes a brand prestigious?

First, there are the Great Houses, as they are known; Swiss watchmakers, some still in the hands of the founding families, who have been making and finishing, by hand, mechanical watches of great precision and complexity for hundreds of years.

Then there are those brands, some equally old, whose names are associated with the great names of jewelry or fashion, whose watches are often made for them by one of the top names, but to whom timekeeping is secondary to beauty. Like the first group, they tend to be very expensive.

Next comes a technological group – not necessarily newcomers – who have decided to follow the electronic path instead, and whose multifunction timepieces are marvels of ingenuity – giving them a prestige all of their own.

Finally, there are a few names whose watches are not in the least expensive, yet whose contribution to the marketing of time has given them an honorable – and indeed prestigious – place in the history of wristwatches.

Frank Edwards

The Story of Watches

Counting the Hours

BELOW
Cleopatra's Needle told time by the shadows it cast.

ABOVE
The Pyramids were used to mark the equinoxes.

The only basis for measuring time in ancient days was the rotation of the earth, and the apparent path of the sun from east to west across the sky was used by the first astronomers to divide the days and nights into regular units.

When humans ceased to be nomadic hunters and began to congregate into communities, they felt the need to split the day into something less vague than sunrise, noon, and sunset. They noticed the differences in the length of shadows cast by the sun, and they erected sticks, and later larger edifices, whose shadow could be measured and related to the passage of time. One of the bigger structures is Cleopatra's Needle, which in 1500 B.C. stood outside a temple at Heliopolis in Egypt, and now stands on the north bank of the River Thames in London. Some of these pillars were used to mark periods of the year – the Great Pyramid in Egypt, designed in part to determine the equinoxes, is an early example; so, too, is Stonehenge in England, erected around 1900 B.C., where on Midsummer's Day, the sun rises over the heelstone at the time of the summer solstice.

Somewhere around 1000 B.C. came the time-sticks of Egypt, T-shaped pieces of wood with raised crosspieces which cast a shadow on the long shaft, which was engraved to mark regular periods of time (the first "hours"). It was placed facing east in the forenoon and had to be reversed in order to face west in the afternoon.

The time-stick was the forerunner of the sundial, also believed to have originated in Egypt, in which a vertical bar called a gnomon cast a shadow on a horizontal dial; later, the stick-like gnomon was replaced by an angled one pointing north and inclined according to the place of origin. The time could then

ABOVE
Pocket sundial. Sundials are believed to have originated in Egypt.

be told not by the length of the shadow but by its direction on the dial, a far more accurate process.

Another early device for measuring the passing hours was the clepsydra, or water-clock. Said to have originated in China where several different forms were developed, it is known to have been used in Babylon around 1500 B.C. An early type found in the Temple of Amon at Karnak in Egypt consisted of an alabaster bowl with rings and inscriptions on the outside and a small hole near the base. As the water escaped, the falling level could be made to show the hours. The outflow hole consisted of a drilled gemstone set into the alabaster – not unlike a jeweled bearing in a modern wristwatch.

But although water-clocks were not particularly handy objects, it took several centuries for their successor as timing device to develop. Sand- or hour-glasses first appeared in the 13th century; an early illustration shows two glass bulbs bound together at the necks; a pierced diaphragm restricted the flow of sand from the upper to the lower, and by measuring out the sand, the time taken could be controlled. They were relatively easy to make, they were portable, and they were fundamentally more accurate than water-clocks.

Sandglasses were the industrial timers of the earliest factories; they were invaluable at sea where, suspended from the ceiling, they operated well even when the sea was rough; and they were a common sight on pulpits in churches.

But they were counters – they did not tell the time.

LEFT
The ancient clock in Salisbury Cathedral, England.

MECHANICAL CLOCKS

It is not known precisely when the mechanical clock, the first instrument for actually telling the time, was invented. Early clocks usually had only one hand and were known as horloges, from the Roman name for a water-clock – *horologium*; those with a bell for tolling the hours were called clocca. Quite large, they were usually made for a church, and they stood on the floor; later models were installed in a tower.

When dial and hands were added to the church clocks, the mechanism to achieve the display of the time of day was often separate from the striking part and was called the "watch." These tower clocks were driven by weights, and it was not until a coiled spring was introduced as the source of power that smaller clocks became a practical proposition.

DOMESTIC CLOCKS

Now began the era of domestic clocks, the first of which were probably the lantern clocks used by watchmen, who hung them on hooks on the wall when not in use. Soon they merited a permanent place on the wall, and it became fashionable to build wooden cases around them and mount them on brackets. By 1600 they were being made of brass instead of iron, which had the effect of making them smaller still and moving them out of the province of the blacksmith and into the hands of the skilled clockmaker.

Then in 1657, a Dutch astronomer and physicist named Christian Huygens devised the pendulum clock. The idea was taken up enthusiastically by English clockmakers, led by Ahasuerus Fromanteel, who was the first to obtain the right to use the idea.

The next step in the evolution of the domestic clock came about when the rich traveler in his carriage wished to know the time. These so-called "carriage" clocks, which the French became especially skilled at making, were mainly of brass and were housed in rectangular cases; they frequently incorporated repeating striking mechanisms so that the owner could tell the time in the dark by pressing a knob on the top.

THE PERSONAL TIMEPIECE

In 1511 a young German locksmith named Peter Henlein built the first really portable personal timekeeper using a small coiled spring – much as he used in his locks – and a scaled-down train of gears. They called it the "Nuremburg Egg." This timekeeper – now called a "watch" – inspired craftsmen all over Europe, especially in Geneva, where a flood of refugees from France and Germany, many of whom

LEFT
The Armorial Bearings of the Worshipful Company of Clockmakers.

were watch- and clockmakers, were fleeing religious persecution and sought refuge in the free city, to whose inhabitants they taught their craft.

Watchmaking soon became one of Switzerland's most important industries, spreading eastward along the Jura Mountains as far as La Chaux de Fonds and Neuchâtel. Some of these early watches were wound by a key through their one hand (clocks with two hands had only been in existence for about 25 years) and had a bow at 12 o'clock through which passed the ribbon or chain by which they were suspended. At this stage, in 1675, Christian Huygens, the man who had invented the pendulum clock, introduced the spiral hairspring, which made for greater accuracy and facilitated the introduction of a minute hand.

ABOVE
Thomas Tompion (1639–1713).

It was about this time, too, that men took to wearing waistcoats. What was more natural than to slip one's watch into a vest pocket instead of hanging it around one's neck?

The next hundred years was the golden age of English horology, which saw the work of some of the greatest clockmakers of all time (most of whom were equally at home making watches). They include Robert Hooke (1635–1703), Thomas Tompion (1639–1713), George Graham (1673–1751), John Harrison (1693–1776), and Thomas Mudge (1715–1794).

BELOW
John Harrison (1693–1776).

Mudge had been working on an idea for an anchor escapement for watches similar to the one used so successfully in pendulum clocks. In 1759 he made first a bracket clock and then a watch with a lever escapement, said to be the most important invention to watchmaking after the balance spring.

Another far-reaching development then took place. Up till then, the pivots of the train had run in metal bearings, resulting in wear and loss of accuracy. A Swiss living in England conceived the idea of using a ruby as a bearing, both at the end of the pivots, and pierced as a bearing in the plate – a technique which the English not only took up with enthusiasm, but kept to themselves. It vastly improved the smooth running of the watches and therefore their accuracy.

Switzerland, too, had its innovative watchmakers. Foremost among them was Abraham-Louis Breguet (1747–1823), whose contributions to horology include the self-winding watch – an invention first conceived by Abraham-Louis Perrelet around 1770; a shock protection

RIGHT
Abraham-Louis Breguet, born 1747.

system; and the tourbillon, a device to offset the effects of gravity on a watch's performance.

From the last quarter of the eighteenth century to the end of the nineteenth, pocket watches became more and more sophisticated. Specialist firms which made only parts grew up; others concentrated on movements, while a third group known as *établisseurs* assembled the various components into complete watches.

The period also saw the founding of some of Switzerland's Great Houses, headed by Vacheron Constantin in 1755, Blancpain, Jaeger-LeCoultre, Longines, Cartier, and IWC, who belonged to that elite band of producers known as manufacturers who made every part of their watches, including the movements, themselves.

Watches became more complicated, incorporating repeaters, phases of the moon, perpetual calendars, and chronographs, but they still tended to be rather bulky, with their movements protected by double cases (which were known as "hunters") which had a hinged cover over the glass.

Then came a development which was to change the design of the personal timekeeper forever.

BELOW
Logos of the Great Swiss Houses.

JAEGER-LECOULTRE
Cartier
JB 1735
BLANCPAIN
IWC
LONGINES
VACHERON CONSTANTIN

BELOW
Grande Complication hunter watch (1889).

The Wristwatch

Just when the wristwatch was invented and by whom is not quite clear. Company archives show that Breguet made a watch for the Queen of Naples in 1810; watch No. 2639 was "designed to be worn on the wrist." Patek Philippe had created a watch with a diameter of only 8.46mm for the famous Crystal Palace Exhibition of 1861; the firm then made a wristwatch for Countess Kocewicz based on the design in 1868, but it was nearly fifty years before the company produced a commercially viable model. In 1886, Girard Perregaux received an order for watches for the officers of the Imperial German Navy. In 1904, Louis Cartier produced a wristwatch for his friend Alberto Santos-Dumont, a Brazilian aviator, in response to a request for a timepiece more convenient than any currently available to use when piloting his airship. By the early 1900s, a number of firms were in production, but all were rather expensive because there was such a large amount of hand craftsmanship in a watch.

WATCHES FOR THE MASSES

It was largely due to some American manufacturers that wristwatches were made available to ordinary people. Around 1850, a group of American watch companies got together with the idea of making a timekeeper for the masses. After the Industrial Revolution, machinery had become much more sophisticated, and the idea was to make thousands of

FAR LEFT
The first wristwatch – made for Countess Kosewicz in 1868.

LEFT
Cartier Santos Dumont Watch.

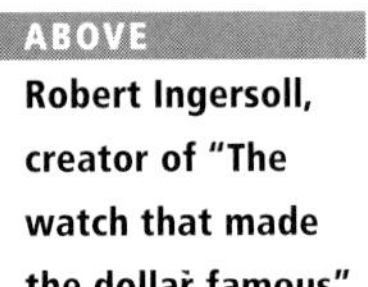

ABOVE
Robert Ingersoll, creator of "The watch that made the dollar famous".

LEFT
The world's first inexpensive wristwatch.

identical interchangeable parts which could be assembled by cheap labor, an idea later used by Henry Ford to produce his Model-Ts. After several false starts, the Waterbury Clock Company succeeded in producing a watch that sold for $3.50. But their ambition was to get the price down to $1.00.

The first man to do so was Robert Ingersoll who, with his brother Charles, ran a mail-order business; every item in their catalog sold for a dollar. Ingersoll persuaded the Waterbury Clock Company to make him a small clock movement by giving them an order – quite considerable in those days – for 12,000 units. He housed them in a case he designed himself. His first models sold, with a chain, for $1.50. They were so successful that, two years later, he went back to Waterbury with an order for half a million pieces; he sold them for $1.00. He had reached his ambition to sell a watch for a day's pay, and christened his product "The watch that made the dollar famous."

LEFT
The Ingersoll Dollar Watch.

By the early 1900s, the line included a petite ladies' model called the Midget. When the demand came for inexpensive wristwatches for the armed forces, it was easy to solder a pair of wire lugs at 12 and 6 o'clock and run a strap across the back; the world's first inexpensive wristwatch was born! It still had the crown on top, but when that was later moved to 3 o'clock, it looked just like its more expensive counterpart. Ingersoll's other innovation was to devise a form of luminous paint which was applied to hands

RIGHT

Ad for Ingersoll Radiolite Watch, c. 1915.

and numerals so that the troops could see the time in the dark. He christened his invention "Radiolite." The use of radium compounds to achieve luminosity was subsequently banned on health grounds.

The idea of using machinery to make accurate and interchangeable parts was not confined to inexpensive watches. Many prestigious Swiss companies took up the idea and improved the quantity and extent of their output without jeopardizing quality, because the parts were still assembled meticulously by hand. The English watchmakers on the other hand declined to have anything to do with these ideas from the New World, and in consequence the English watch industry went into a decline from which it never recovered.

England had previously had a thriving watch industry in the middle of the 19th century with centers at Liverpool, Coventry, and London. In 1858, the British Horologial Institution was formed to protect the interest of its clock- and watchmaking members, largely against foreign competition. They were aware of the American ideas and knew that European companies were following the American lead, but the British continued to complain about competition from cheap labor while not realizing that the future lay in increasing mechanization. Watchmaking in England was still a cottage industry whose practitioners failed to realize that the competition had moved on.

It was apparent to the Swiss that the secret lay in the quality of the machine tools employed. Many firms already employed engineers of the highest caliber. Georges-August Lechot, for instance, had designed and built a range of machines for Vacheron Constantin that revolutionized the firm's production as far back as 1843. But because the majority of Swiss watches at that time were of the better-quality jeweled-lever variety, they were still relatively expensive.

American companies were not the only ones to have considered the possibility of making a cheap watch for the masses. In the middle of the 19th century, a German watchmaker named Georges-Frédéric Roskopf working in La Chaux de Fonds decided he could make a watch for 20 francs. He set about simplifying the escapement; he eliminated a

VIGILANTIA

Founded 1858

ABOVE

Logo of the British Horological Institute.

number of parts and replaced the jewels in the lever by pins. He modified the winding and cheapened the case. Much to the surprise of the industry, he received a bronze medal at the Paris Exhibition of 1868. One hundred years later, the Swiss were exporting 28 million "Roskopf" watches a year and were the world's leading suppliers of cheap watches.

Traditional watchmakers did not think much of Roskopf's watches to start with – and initially many were of poor manufacture – but as production became more refined, pin-lever watches achieved a respectable quality in relation to their price. One Swiss manufacturer, Oris, entered pin-lever watches in an official trial and received a certificate of chronometer quality, much to the chagrin of the jeweled-lever fraternity.

RÉPUBLIQUE ET CANTON DE
NEUCHATEL (SUISSE)

OBSERVATOIRE ASTRONOMIQUE
ET CHRONOMÉTRIQUE

BULLETIN DE MARCHE

Le soussigné certifie que le chronomètre N° — 681 —

diamètre: 25.5 mm échappement: ancre à cheville
spiral: Nivarox balancier: monométallique

de

ORIS WATCH Co., S.A.,
HOLSTEIN a subi les épreuves pour

CHRONOMÈTRES-BRACELET

conformément au règlement (voir au verso) et a donné les résultats suivants :

Ecart moyen de la marche diurne . . . . . E = ± 0.20 s
Coefficient thermique . . . . . C = − 0.022
Erreur secondaire de la compensation . . . . . S = + 3.21
Reprise de marche (périodes 1 et 10) . . . . . R = + 0.20
Variation des marches moyennes du plat au pendu . . . . . − 0.73
Variation des marches moyennes du cadran en haut au cadran en bas . . . − 0.72
Ecart moyen correspondant à un changement de position . . . . P = ± 1.65

Neuchâtel,.. le 30 avril 1968

Le directeur de l'Observatoire,

Les chronomètres sont comparés tous les jours à l'horloge fondamentale de l'Observatoire, au moyen d'un chronographe-enregistreur.
Le signe + indique l'avance, le signe — le retard.

ABOVE
Official Certificate of "Chronometer" quality.

In 1923 John Harwood produced the first self-winding wristwatch. The system had originally been devised by Perrelet for pocket watches in 1770, but in spite of the popularity of the wristwatch, no one had previously thought of applying the principle to them. With no English manufacturer to take up his idea, Harwood patented it in Switzerland where it was swiftly adopted, notably by the Rolex Watch Company, which was in production with a perpetual self-winding wristwatch by 1931.

By the 1960s the watch industry in the middle and upper price ranges was virtually dominated by the Swiss, and they could be forgiven for thinking that the watch had reached its zenith. Firms like Audemars Piguet, IWC, and Patek Philippe were creating complicated timepieces with a multiplicity of functions, hand-finished to an incredible degree of accuracy, and housed in fabulous 18-karat gold cases engraved and embellished with precious gems. What more could one want? The exciting answer was just over the horizon.

RIGHT
Rolex self-wind. The movement is wound at the slightest action of the wrist.

GREENWICH MEAN TIME

Here it is necessary to go back in time to establish the background. If timepieces are to be usefully accurate, they have to be related to some agreed common point – a timely benchmark.

Thanks to the work of other English clockmakers, John Harrison's work on ship's chronometers was carried to greater lengths. John Arnold, George Graham, and Thomas Earnshaw all contributed to the improvement of the design; so too, did Pierre Le Roy, a Frenchman whose major contribution was the

LEFT
Audemars Piguet – Grande Complication.

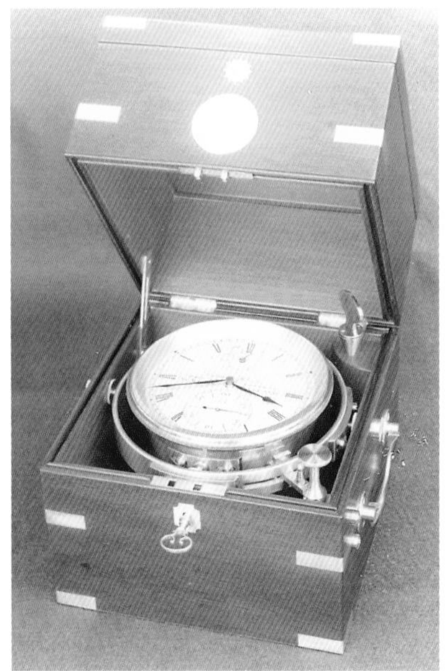

ABOVE
By the 19th century, marine chronometers had achieved a high degree of accuracy.

compensated balance which he made of two dissimilar metals to overcome the effect of temperature changes. By the nineteenth century, marine chronometers had achieved a high degree of accuracy, but there remained the need for some sort of time signal by which they could be set.

John Pond, the Astronomer Royal, solved the problem in 1833 by installing a time ball at Greenwich Observatory. It was a wooden ball about three feet in diameter which slid up and down a 15-foot high mast. Just before 1 o'clock each day, it was wound up to the top of the mast; at 01.00 hours precisely it was dropped by a trigger mechanism; later an electrical device was connected to it so that the Observatory's Mean Solar Time clock could release it automatically. Time balls were subsequently installed at all the major ports – and a time ball was also erected in the Strand, London for the benefit of the chronometer makers who worked there.

But different towns still kept different local times. In 1880, Mean Solar Time at Greenwich was legally established as Britain's official time. In 1884 an international conference decided to adopt the meridian through Greenwich as zero and to use Greenwich Mean Time as the basis for a global system. The world was divided into 24 time zones, each one hour apart; only Ireland and France opposed the proposition, which was nevertheless adopted.

Electricity was a boon to the distribution of time. Big Ben was linked to Greenwich by the electric telegraph for time checks, as was the Post Office, still today a vital link in the supply of time. Shortly after World War I, an American named Henry Ellis Warren invented the synchronous clock which he called the Telechron. It operated from the main electricity supply – and to that extent was only as accurate as the stability of the frequency – but it was another step forward (though strictly speaking, it was not a clock but an electric motor). In Britain the firm of S. Smith & Sons took up the idea and became the biggest manufacturer of synchronous clocks. Unfortunately, World War II caused fluctuations in electricity supply and affected sales for a number of years. It was not until the mid-50s that mains electricity was stable enough for people to trust synchronous clocks again.

But an alternative had already appeared. Both the French and German clock industries had been working on battery clocks. One version, designed by Kienzle, was an ordinary mechanical clock with a light mainspring which was rewound every 15 minutes by a battery which operated a solenoid. The system provided a relatively constant drive, and hence good timekeeping. Such clocks were ideal in the house for they required little attention; they were also quickly adapted for use in the car as dashboard clocks since battery power was readily available; both Keinzle and Smiths developed automotive subsidiaries that are still in existence today.

With the invention in 1948 of the transistor, electric clocks became more reliable still, but the chief effect was to point the way to the next development – the electronic timekeeper.

RIGHT

In 1833 a time ball was installed at Greenwich Observatory.

The first electronic timepiece ever produced was built in 1929 by W. A. Morrison, a Canadian working in the United States. It was about the size of a small room and was based on the principle that a piece of quartz crystal cut in a certain way will resonate at a fixed frequency if an electric current is applied to it. In other words, it behaves like an extremely rapidly vibrating balance wheel. A subsequent development was the atomic clock, based on the vibrations of an atom of cesium, which are several million times faster than those of a quartz crystal. Said to be accurate to within one second in 3,000 years, it is rather impractical for everyday use, but is the basis for National Time in Britain and elsewhere; the signals are used for accurate time-setting internationally and for navigational purposes. Britain broadcasts time signals from the Post Office clock at Rugby, and the U.S.A. from Fort Collins, Colorado; other transmitters are located in Nagasaki, Japan, and Frankfurt, Germany.

RADIO-CONTROLLED TIME

We have seen how the electric telegraph enabled time signals to be widely circulated from Greenwich. In the 1980s a German firm, Junghans, developed a radio-controlled clock which operated from time signals transmitted from the national transmitters referred to above. These signals include both time and

BELOW
Junghans Radio controlled watch

date information so that adjustments for leap years, short months, and seasonal time changes are made automatically. In the Junghans clock the receiver is activated every hour. The firm's next innovation was to cram the technology into a wristwatch, with the reception antenna hidden in the strap. The Mega wristwatch series is corrected once a day; since the seconds display is digital – and that is all that will normally need correcting – the system is even simpler than that of the clocks.

THE FIRST ELECTRIC WATCH

In 1952 Fred Lip, a French watch manufacturer, produced the prototype of a watch powered by a battery; working with the Elgin Company of America, he tried to manufacture them, but few were actually produced. The first genuinely electronic watch incorporating a transistorized circuit was designed by a Swiss engineer, Max Hetzel. However, finding no support for his idea in his own country, he took it to Bulova in the United States who marketed it. It was called the Tuning Fork module because the shape of its oscillator was similar to a tuning fork.

A number of Swiss manufacturers then banded together to finance the research and development of a quartz oscillator. The Centre for Electric Horology in Neuchâtel produced the first quartz-based movement; it was called Beta I. It won first prize in a competition organized by the Centre, with a prototype from Seiko taking second place.

Seiko was no stranger to the technology, having already produced a large quartz chronometer to time the 1964 Olympic Games; in 1968 the firm entered a wristwatch version for the Centre's competition and the following year launched the world's first commercially viable quartz wristwatch, the Astron.

Meanwhile, in the United States, a number of large companies involved in the space program had

RIGHT
Seiko Astron c.1969.

developed calculator modules to display digital time. An obvious disadvantage was that, in order to see the time, the user had to press a button on the side of the case. To obviate this, Ebauches SA in Switzerland and Texas Instruments in California joined forces to develop a liquid crystal (LCD) display whose readout was permanently visible. The problem was that both these systems drained their tiny batteries very rapidly.

RIGHT
The first Ingersoll Analogue Quartz, 1975.

In Switzerland and Japan, companies concentrated on producing watches with "normal" faces – with a dial and hands – and by using stepping motors translated the vibrations of the quartz crystal into a rotary motion to turn the hands. The "Analog" system became the universal one for better-quality watches.

The outstanding aspect of the new timepieces was their incredible accuracy – but they still had the drawback of needing to have the battery replaced – even though the latest type of lithium battery can last up to ten years. So two firms decided to do away with batteries altogether. The Seiko Kinetic model employs a tiny rotor, much like a mechanical automatic, which uses the wearer's movements to generate electricity into a specially designed capacitor which acts as a reservoir, storing power until it is needed. It is so efficient that, once it is fully charged, the watch will operate for 14 days without being worn. It was launched in 1993 after twenty years of development.

An entirely different system is embodied in the Citizen Eco-Drive, which uses advanced ceramics on the dial that allow light to pass through; light falls on a photo-electric cell which converts it into electrical energy; it gains enough energy from one minute of daylight or 15 minutes of artificial light to run the watch for 24 hours. The energy is stored in a secondary battery which releases it as required; once it is fully charged, it will power the watch for between two to six months depending on the model, without having to be exposed again to light.

In a further refinement, Junghans, which had also been developing solar technology, combined this with the radio system in its Mega-Solar-Ceramic model. The case is made from a zirconium oxide ceramic with the antenna placed in it; the solar system when fully charged – which takes 30 minutes of bright light – will run for up to six months even in darkness and is corrected, like the original Mega watch, by the nearest national radio transmitter.

So the wheel has neatly come full circle, and the sun, which first allowed ancient peoples to mark the passage of time, now operates the most technologically advanced electronic timepieces.

LEFT
Citizen Ecodrive

Directory of Watches

Types of Watches

The mechanical watch consists of three elements:

- A source of power – the mainspring
- A series of toothed wheels – the train – which transmits that power
- A regulating mechanism comprising a balance wheel and hairspring, and an escapement.

Mechanical watches have either jeweled-lever or pin-lever escapements; a variation of the latter is the Roskopf escapement used mainly in cheaper constructions. The escapement is located between an oscillator – the balance wheel – and the gear-train; the lever version was invented by Thomas Mudge and remains virtually the same today as in his day.

The crown (winder) winds the mainspring; as it unwinds, the toothed rim of its casing (the barrel) sets in motion the wheels of the train, which act on the hands to show the time. The most important part of this operation is controlling the transmission of power so that it is even and regular.

For reliably accurate measurement, time must be divided into absolutely equal parts; the briefer they are, the more precise the measurement. The balance wheel rotates a half-revolution one way before being pulled up by the hairspring at its center, when it proceeds to rotate in the opposite direction. This oscillation chops the action into equal parts and creates the familiar "tick-tock" sound of mechanical watches. These half-oscillations are called vibrations and are known as the beat; a normal watch beats at 18,000 vibrations per hour; a very high frequency movement has 36,000 vph.

Each movement of the balance wheel acts on an anchor-shaped lever which frees one tooth at a time of the escape wheel. Thus the power of the mainspring is turned into a rhythmic series of movements, which end up – via the reduction gears – at the hands to show the time.

Jewels are fitted wherever friction occurs; they used to be rubies, but are now man-made corundum. The jewels of a jeweled-lever watch are situated at the ends of the lever; in a pin-lever watch, they are replaced by hardened steel pins.

An ordinary mechanical watch has about 130 parts, situated between the bottom plate and the bridges which keep them together.

Movements come in various sizes measured in millimeters or lignes,

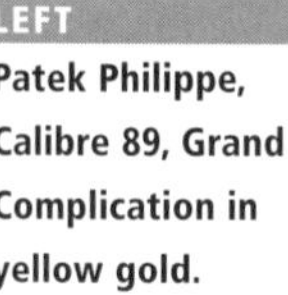

LEFT

Patek Philippe, Calibre 89, Grand Complication in yellow gold.

with 1 ligne = 2.25mm. To distinguish movements of the same size by different makers, the term "caliber" is always employed.

Automatic watches are operated by the action of a rotor, which winds the watch through the wearer's movements. The advantage, in addition to not having to wind the watch every day, is that the mainspring is kept fully wound so the power output – and thus the rate of the watch – is constant.

Chronographs, or stopwatches, are watches with a stop/start facility which enables the wearer to time an event and count the lapsed time in seconds, minutes, and hours. The mechanism is operated by a slide or knob on the side of the case. A rattrapante (or flyback) chronograph has two center seconds hands, which can be operated separately to time two competitors at once. Most chronographs time to ⅕th second: the main mechanism keeps running when the center seconds hands fly back to zero.

Chronometers are very high-quality watches which have undergone stringent individual tests at the official testing station, the Contrôle Official Suisse des Chronomètres. When it passes the tests, each watch is awarded a certificate.

Phases of the moon are astronomically predictable, as are leap years, so they can be programed into a watch mechanism; provided the watch is not stopped, they can go on into the next century.

Grande complications are pocket or wristwatches which combine telling time with every known function: perpetual calendars, moonphases, stop/start mechanisms, alarms, repeaters, strikes, and even thermometers. A typical example by Patek Philippe is an astronomical pocket watch with tourbillon escapement which has 33 functions, 1,728 working parts, and took four years to assemble.

THE ELECTRONIC WATCH

Like its mechanical counterpart, the electronic watch has a power source, a regulator, and a system to display the time, either digitally or by means of hands and a dial.

The power source is a battery. Its current is conveyed to an integrated circuit – the regulator – which accepts the vibrations of a quartz oscillator and transforms them into impulses which conform to an agreed frequency, now universally accepted as 32,768 Hertz, or vibrations per second. Because electronic oscillations are of a very much higher order than those of a mechanical balance, which at maximum is 36,000 vph, it became necessary to devise a new standard; the Hertz, corresponding to one vibration per second, was chosen. Impulses are either fed into a stepping motor which drives a train of gears to activate the hands, or processed by the integrated circuit driver section to command a liquid crystal display (LCD).

The batteries used today are silver oxide or the longer-lasting lithium type. Analog models usually need only one battery, which can last from two to five or even ten years depending on the model.

The oscillator is a piezoelectric quartz crystal cut by laser to an exact predetermined shape to give the required frequency of 32,768Hz.

The integrated circuit (IC) is more often than not of the CMOS-LS type.

The stepping motor transforms the impulses from the driver part of the IC into a rotating or rocking motion. Original motors were capable only of driving the hands and a date display; modern complicated quartz watches employ up to four stepping motors in order to drive their multiple functions.

Solar cells are sometimes fitted to quartz watches to transform light into electrical energy, which can then be stored in a form of accumulator.

Liquid crystals combine a liquid and a solid state. Elongated molecules arranged parallel to each other can be switched from vertical to horizontal positions by stimulation from an electric current, like a venetian blind being opened and closed. Vertical molecules are transparent and admit light; in the horizontal position, they are opaque and reflect light, with the reflection appearing as a black area. The liquid crystals are layered between very thin glass plates bearing a grid of electrodes which form the seven segments needed to form the figures 0 to 9.

The driver section of the IC determines which segments are to be activated, in what order, and for how long, to form the appropriate figures.

The variety of functions (which are really programs) provided by digital watches entails the use of far more complicated ICs than those found in analog quartz watches, and some modern models incorporate a microprocessor, as the detailed descriptions of some of the watches in the Directory will show.

MOVEMENTS

Apart from the elite Swiss firms which make their own movements, most watch manufacturers buy their movements from specialist firms, the largest of which is ETA Fabrique d'Ebauches at Grenchen. This 200-year-old company is now part of SMH (Societé Suisse de Microélectronique et d'Horlogerie) and owns factories in Switzerland, France, Germany, Malaysia, and Taiwan. It turns out 100 million movements a year, three-quarters of which are quartz. The movements come in a series of "families," based on size, quality, or price. Its mechanical movements are of a high quality, a typical example being the Valjou 7750 chronograph movement used by so many well-known brands.

ETA's movements, both quartz and mechanical, are also supplied to the house brands of SMH – Omega, Longines, Rado, and Tissot.

Other sources of movements in Switzerland are Ronda, an old-established family firm in Lengnau, and ISA, which specializes in ultrathin quartz movements for the top end of the trade. The big Japanese firms not only make their own movements, but also supply other carefully selected manufacturers.

ABOVE
Logo of ETA Fabrique d'Ebauches

FEATURES

Luminous watches: As a result of a demand from the Army in World War I, dials and hands were often painted with luminous substances so the wearer could tell time in the dark. An earlier substance contained zinc sulfide agitated by a radioactive salt. This potentially dangerous material was banned in the 1950s and has now been replaced by tritium, a substance with very low radioactivity, the amount of which is monitored and controlled by ISO standards.

Recently, other means of illuminating the time in the dark have been devised. The Timex Indiglo system is based on electroluminescence; pressing a button on the side of the case activates a minute current from the battery, which excites electrodes on the dial material which then give off energy in the form of light. An alternative system has a dial coated with fluorescent material which is activated after a short period of exposure to any source of light, after which it will last for another eight hours.

ABOVE
Timex Indiglo

Power reserve: The idea of having an indication of the power remaining in the mainspring was first devised by Breguet and has appeared in various guises ever since. The latest ETA movement, for instance, incorporates a power reserve indicator as a matter of course.

Shock protection is now universal; most good watches use Incabloc, a system derived from Breguet's original *parachut*. To be called shock-proof, a watch must meet conditions set out in International Standard 1413, which include two blows on the case equivalent to a one-meter (1 yard) drop onto a hard surface, after which it must not show a variation in rate of more than 60 seconds a day.

Most watches now claim to be antimagnetic. A mechanical watch can be thrown off balance if it comes in contact with a strong magnetic field, and magnetism is a common factor of daily life – in motor cars, hi-fi systems, refrigerators, etc. To overcome the effect, alloys are used for the balance wheel, escape wheel, and other parts. A watch can be described as anti-magnetic if it does not stop after exposure to a magnetic field of 4900 amps per meter and subsequently does not deviate by more than 30 seconds per day. The majority of better-class watches qualify: if special protection is needed, a watch like the IWC Ingenieur is called for. Its movement is housed in a complete alloy jacket inside the normal case, and even the dial is made of antimagnetic soft iron.

Electronic watches are not susceptible to magnetism nor, since they have fewer parts than mechanical watches and no balance staff, do they need a special shockproof device.

Most watches these days are water-resistant. The patents protecting the original screwdown crown have long since expired, and accurate machining means that cases can easily be made relatively water-resistant. To go underwater to great depths presents another problem, requiring special gaskets and even helium valves as in the Breitling Superocean. But the main advantage of water-resistance is that it also keeps out the dust – and dust is the enemy of delicate mechanisms. Watches which are used for serious diving – 100 feet or more – must be checked regularly and the gaskets replaced by a qualified person. The only accepted description is Water-Resistant – waterproof is no longer allowed internationally.

The crystal, often still called the glass (although ordinary glass has not been used for many years), is made from either acrylic plastic, a rugged compound which does not yellow with age and can be cut, molded, or injected, or mineral glass, a natural glass chemically treated to form a tempered hard outer coating resistant to knocks and scratches. The very best watches have sapphire crystals, a man-made corundum with the hardness of real sapphire. It is, to all intents and purposes, scratchproof and is especially preferred for the see-through backs of complicated watches.

RIGHT
Breitling Superocean

The Hallmarks of a Good Watch

Since the prime function of a watch is to tell the time, the first test of a good watch is its accuracy, and the length of time it can maintain that. In this regard, quartz watches are paramount, with an accuracy that is never less than a few seconds a month and an ability to maintain that almost indefinitely. The solar-powered models take their energy from the sun and do not even need their batteries replaced.

LEFT
Junghan's Mega Solar Ceramic

Mechanical watches, even the very best hand-built models, rarely achieve an accuracy to rival the performance of quartz. But a good mechanical automatic with tourbillon, which compensates for the effect of gravity, will give a precision adequate for the average owner, and some with perpetual calendar are programed as far ahead as the year 2000. Most, too, have a power reserve of more than 40 hours, which means that, over 24 hours, the rate of going of the watch will be absolutely constant.

ABOVE
Patek Philippe rose gold watch, ultra thin, with mechanical movement.

The next factor is appearance. Much attention is paid to the design and finish of dials, which in a good watch are often gold or silver, delicately engraved, and with appliqué numbers or batons in 18-karat gold and hands made of matching material. The dial should blend harmoniously with the case.

Cases may be of precious metal – gold in various colors, pink, rose, yellow, or white, usually 18-karat, which is harder than the best quality of 24-karat. Platinum is popular; silver is occasionally used. Employing precious metal considerably affects the price of the watch; the case and bracelet, if that too is in precious metal, usually cost far more than even the most intricate handmade movements.

RIGHT
Maurice Lacroix – a selection of ladies elegant bi-color bracelet watches

Stainless steel is becoming more popular now that case makers are learning to apply different finishes, such as brushed, or satin finish, often alternating this with a high polish.

Bicolor cases – those using steel and gold in combination – are proving attractive, especially in ladies' models. It should be noted that in Britain it is illegal to describe a bicolor watch as "gold" and steel; it has to be called "yellow metal" unless it *is* gold, when it will be hallmarked and the jeweler may describe it verbally as gold.

Finally, the most reliable hallmark of a good watch is the name. The best watches are known the world over. They are guaranteed, sometimes up to five years, and often provide an international list of service agents. And they will be sold in a reputable jeweler's shop or the jewelry department of a reputable store.

Counterfeiting of watches is big business worldwide. To make sure you buy a good watch, follow three simple rules. Go to a reliable jeweler or store, pick a well-known brand, and insist on a guarantee and a receipt that clearly states the quality of the precious metal (18-karat gold, or gold plate), the brand name, and any special features.

Don't forget, good watches are never sold in bars, in garage sales, in flea markets, or from "friends of friends" in the trade.

WHAT MAKES A GOOD WATCH EXPENSIVE?

In a cheap and cheerful plastic quartz watch that just tells the time, there are anything from 50 to 100 parts, produced automatically and assembled robotically. It is rugged and dependable, and will give good service. But every additional feature adds to the cost. A date? A day date? The movement requires more parts, and the assembly takes a little longer. A water-protected case, a glare-proof sapphire crystal – they all add up.

Then there are the mechanical watches, the ones usually collected by connoisseurs. Remember, Swatch is one of the few quartz watches that are collectors' pieces and then only in special editions. There are more parts to start with in a mechanical watch and they are rather more delicate. Things like a balance wheel have to be poised, the balance spring adjusted, the torque of the mainspring checked. Add a rotor to make it automatic, a train of gears for the calendar work, and you are starting to get quite a collection of tiny bits and pieces which have to be assembled mainly by hand, even with the aid of jigs and other mechanical devices. Now look at what are known as Complications. A Patek Philippe model can consist of over 1,000 parts.

It takes a skilled watchmaker anything from nine months to two years to assemble; it undergoes innumerable tests of each subassembly along the way, long before the movement is complete and ready to be put in its case.

If, for instance, the case is an 18-karat gold Rolex Oyster (or platinum or stainless steel), it requires over 100 operations to turn from a solid block of gold into a perfectly finished case. It then takes a further 35 operations to make and fit the famous Oyster waterproof crown.

After the movement is put into the case, further tests have to be carried out to make sure it is protected from dust and water and shocks. That can take a week.

ABOVE
The famous Rolex Oyster case.

LEFT
Jaeger-LeCoultre – Master Lady

RIGHT
Swatch spring/summer 1996 – The Artists

In the case of the Jaeger-LeCoultre Master series, it takes 1,000 hours – or roughly three weeks. And if it is a chronometer, it has to be sent to the official Swiss testing authority (COSC) for a further 15 days of tests before it can obtain its certificate, just a piece of paper to the new owner, but a guarantee of performance that had to be earned.

Add up all those hours of skilled work, the cost of the raw ingredients – the ingot of gold, the block of steel to make the case – and you can see why good watches are expensive. And we haven't even looked at the diamond-studded ones!

WATCHES AS STATUS SYMBOLS

A watch is one of the few pieces of jewelry worn by both men and women. It can tell the observer a lot about the owner. Many people regard the watch as purely functional. They need to know the time – to catch trains or aircraft, to attend meetings, even just to see a television program. Since nothing in our daily lives ever goes to within half a minute of its advertised time, extreme accuracy is irrelevant however.

ABOVE
Ladies 18kt gold Datejust

LEFT
Patek Philippe watches

What is needed, though, of course, is reliability – if possible year in, year out.

For everyday wear, men tend to choose large watches, with complicated dials, several knobs, and frequently a matching bracelet. Since some of the better-known brands use personalities in their advertisements, it is regarded as a status symbol to wear an 18-karat gold Rolex Datejust as worn by a famous explorer or sportsman – in other words, a sign of undeniable good taste.

There is a tendency among some of the elite brands to offer men's models with diamond-set bezels and even bracelets. It could be argued that men who wear them are making a very personal statement about their status, perhaps a risky one in view of rising figures of robbery from the person.

For the more retiring, there is an increasing trend, especially for evening wear, for a very slim gold watch on a crocodile strap as a symbol of understated luxury.

LEFT

Truly feminine – Cartier Mini Baignoire with "on the cloud" bracelet in yellow gold and diamonds, dial in white mother-of-pearl mosaic.

RIGHT

Distinct man-appeal – Breitling chronograph "crosswind"

The slimmer and the more delicate the watch, the higher the price.

Many women enjoy wearing diamonds, and their timepieces are no exception. Most of the top manufacturers have a *Haute Joaillerie* collection ranging from a modest diamond on the dial to one completely set with brilliants on bezel and bracelet. Sometimes even the dial is paved with tiny gems. Whether or not the time can be read is immaterial. The point is that the wearer's status has been projected.

STARTING A COLLECTION

The first thing to do in starting a collection – of anything, not only watches – is to find out all about the subject to save many a false start. There is a host of books on the subject of watches, and auction catalogs from the famous auction houses like Christies, Phillips, Sothebys and Antiquorum in Geneva are a valuable source of information about what is available and at what price. They can, however, be expensive to buy.

Visiting auction rooms is also useful. There are lots of watches on display, and the sale-room staff is usually most helpful; they are also experts worth listening to. If at all possible, go to previews and then to the auction to allow you to compare estimates with actual prices paid. It will also help you get a better feel for the market.

The next thing to decide is what you are going to collect. There are literally hundreds of different types of watches – men's, women's, pocket, wrist, plain, complicated, sports, dress, and so on. It helps to concentrate your sights on a small area to begin with – you can always enlarge it. If you go too wide at first, you may find yourself trying to sell off unwanted items before you've really got started.

You should also study up-to-date magazines relating to watches and clocks. Some are purely trade

BELOW
Ad from the early 1900s for Ingersoll entitled "His first watch."

journals and will give you useful information about current models. Some are available only to members, like *Horological Journal,* the publication of the British Horological Institute. Some are aimed specifically at collectors, like *International WristWatch,* which contains regular articles on auctions and prices, and gives background information about famous brands.

It will also pay to study the history of watches in general. Certain dates are important – the launch of the first wristwatch, for example – since they provide a reference point on which to base your collection. Early quartz models from the 1970s might be interesting – the first Swatches are fetching fabulous prices. But you should try to be original. If your chosen type is too easy to come by, your collection will not be very special. That is why collectors go for limited editions from the Great Houses – they know the model is exclusive right from the start.

Finally, when you do decide to buy, keep everything pertaining to your purchase – not only the receipt, but packaging, guarantee, and certificate (if it is a chronometer) as well. These may be invaluable one day if you decide to sell or to establish the provenance of a particular piece.

There is a Swatch Collectors Club in the UK, but not one for general collectors. However, America has a flourishing one in Columbia, Pennsylvania.

CARE OF WATCHES

A mechanical watch should never, if at all possible, be allowed to stop. Do not think it saves wear and tear if it is stopped. On the contrary, if its moving parts are not in motion, the special oil which lubricates the bearings will eventually dry out and harden. The lubricant may eventually become loaded with dust, to the detriment of the fine mechanism. If you do not use your mechanical watch regularly, wind it at least once a week.

Try to avoid subjecting your watch to sudden changes of temperature. Diving into the pool after having been in the sun, for instance, can cause the moisture in the air inside the watch to condense (particularly in a water-protected case) and seep into the movement; this applies to quartz watches, too, since the circuitry is very susceptible to humidity.

Remember, you have a high precision instrument on your wrist which ticks ten times a second every minute and every hour of the day, 314 million times a year. It is subjected to all sorts of stresses and strains in its daily life. Try not to add to them or create new or unusual ones for it. And do remember to take it to a qualified watchmaker-jeweler for a check-up and re-oil every year or so. That way, it could well last your lifetime.

LEFT
The very first "Mickey Mouse" watch – 1933.

№1

Audemars Piguet

Jules Audemars and Edward Piguet were just 24 and 22 years old respectively when they founded the Audemars Piguet manufactory in 1875 in Le Brassus. With a declared aim to create the finest watches in the world, members of the company's founding families are still on the board of directors, almost a century and a quarter after its inception.

ABOVE

PERPETUAL CALENDAR COLLECTION

With manual winding, this square perpetual calendar contains 21 rubies.

From the beginning the firm specialized in complex watches, producing their first Grande Complication, a gold hunter which had a minute repeater, perpetual calendar, phases of the moon, split-second chronograph, and power reserve indicator, in 1889.

In 1906, soon after wristwatches had been invented, they had already built one with a minute repeater; in 1920 they introduced the world's smallest minute repeater, and five years later the world's thinnest pocket watch with a movement height of only 1.32mm. The next seventy years saw a procession of world "firsts" – all masterpieces in their particular fields and all made with the attention to quality that had been the hallmark of the founders.

ABOVE

MILLENARY

The Millenary Chronometer, showing the elegant simplicity of this line.

Audemars Piguet's current line includes a watch to celebrate the arrival of the third millennium. Called the Millenary, it has a highly unusual case of horizontal oval design, with an original dial to match. It is available as a simple day/date, a perpetual calendar, or a chronograph.

BELOW

ROYAL OAK JUBILEE

Limited Edition Anniversary model, with transparent back and ultra-thin automatic movement.

The Grande Complication automatic wristwatch is a model steeped in the firm's traditions. It has over 600 parts, yet it is only 8.55mm thick; it displays the day, date, month, and phases of the moon, a perpetual calendar which can cope with leap years, a split-second chronograph precise to $^{1}/_{5}$th second, and a minute repeater striking hours, quarters, and minutes as desired.

PRODUCT RANGE

Les Compliqués
Les Classiques
Millenary
Royal Oak
Carnegie

AP
AUDEMARS PIGUET

ABOVE
Jules-Louis Audemars, 1851-1918.

ABOVE
Edward-Auguste Piguet, 1853-1919.

BELOW
The factory of Audemars Piguet in Le Brassus, Vaudois Jura, Vallée de Joux, Switzerland.

For the ladies, Audemars Piguet's latest creation is the Roberta Line – a line of quartz-powered gemset watches with 18-karat gold cases of elegant design enhanced by diamonds, sapphires, and rubies, all of top quality and exquisitely cut.

LEFT
ROBERTA LINE
Haute horlogerie using precious stones and metals, a truly feminine line.

RIGHT

2003 ULTRA THIN is just 1.64mm thick. A limited edition of 300 watches marks the 50th anniversary of this popular watch in 1996.

FACT FILE

FOUNDED: 1875
COUNTRY OF ORIGIN: Switzerland
OUTPUT: 15,000 pieces per annum
MOVEMENT: 70% mechanical, 30% quartz
CEO: Steven Urqhart and Georges-Henri Meylan (Joint Chief Executive Officers)

In contrast to the massive Complication is the Calibre 2003, an ultraslim model in a yellow-gold case on a strap, driven by a quartz movement of Audemars Piguet's own construction.

FLAGSHIP LINE

In 1972 Audemars Piguet launched a line of mechanical watches in steel cases with hexagonal screws fastening the bezel called Royal Oak in honor of the British Royal Navy's famous ships of the line bearing that name. This rugged sportsman's model with its "porthole" motif caught on; the watch became available in yellow or pink gold, with day and date displays, moon-phases, perpetual calendars – it was even fitted with a quartz movement to allow a slimmer profile. There is a Royal Oak Dual Time, whose automatic movement has a 21-karat gold rotor, while the Royal Oak Offshore has a case water-resistant to 10ATM. The latest creation is a Royal Oak Offshore for ladies, which has a smaller "porthole" case and an automatic movement protected from magnetic fields by a special mild steel cage.

ABOVE

The British Royal Navy named three of its most important vessels Royal Oak.

BELOW

ROYAL OAK

The Royal Oak Offshore, water-resistant to 10 ATM, distinctive octagonal porthole and clearly visible screws.

Nº2

BAUME ET MERCIER

In 1542, while watchmaking was in its infancy, the Baume family set up a workshop in Les Bois in the Swiss Jura. Their descendants registered the "Société Baume Frères" in 1834 to manufacture complete watches.

ABOVE
RIVIERA
Trademark 12-sided steel case, leather strap, screw down crown and automatic movement.

From the outset they specialized in chronometers, and the high quality of their work was commented on by the newly formed British Horological Institute. In consequence Pierre-Joseph Baume visited England, decided to stay, and opened a subsidiary in 1878 in London to import and market the firm's watches. By now the company had an international reputation and had won a number of awards, the most prestigious from the Kew Observatory in 1883, for a still unrivaled 91.9% for a chronometer with a tourbillon movement.

In 1918 William Baume joined forces with Paul Mercier, the artistic son of a Czarist officer, and the firm of Baume et Mercier was born in Geneva. His influence was reflected in another rare award – the Poinçon de Genève – which gave the company the right to use the Geneva hallmark. The fortunes of the firm were consistent – if undistinguished – right up to the mid-1950s when the succession petered out. The old-established firm of Piaget took a majority holding, and at once its technical expertise placed Baume et Mercier in a position to market an extremely flat automatic.

But the electronic age had arrived. In 1971 the firm produced one of the first tuning-fork watches, and from then on, quartz technology played an increasing part in their production. The last of their own mechanical movements was made in 1983.

ABOVE
HAMPTON
With distinctive, curved steel case and salmon dial. Automatic movement.

PRODUCT RANGE

Riviera
Hampton
Linea
Ilea
Malibu
Classic

BAUME & MERCIER

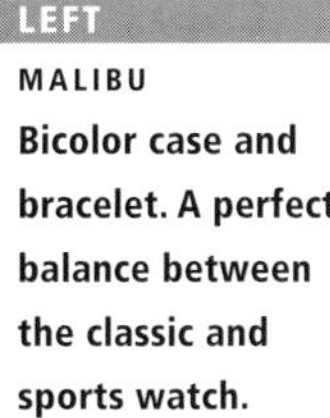

LEFT
MALIBU
Bicolor case and bracelet. A perfect balance between the classic and sports watch.

ABOVE
Delicacy and elegance shown off to perfection – The Ilea collection.

In 1988 both Baume et Mercier and Piaget were acquired by Cartier International; the resources of one of Switzerland's most modern production plants were now at their disposal.

Among Baume et Mercier's current lines, the Hampton, launched two years ago, has been remarkably successful. Its subtly curved case is reminiscent of the Art Deco period. The man's model has an automatic movement, the ladies a quartz; both come with bracelet or strap. The Malibu is a rugged sports watch with heavy bezel and screwdown crown, which in 1996 included a chronograph model with automatic movement; it is water resistant to 300 feet. Linea is a stylish line of ladies fashion watches in gold cases, some gemset, while the Classic collection epitomizes traditional Baume et Mercier production: they are made only in 18-karat gold.

FACT FILE

FOUNDED: 1834
COUNTRY OF ORIGIN: Switzerland
OUTPUT: 100,000 pieces per annum
Worldwide distribution
MOVEMENT: 70% quartz, 30% mechanical
CEO: Eugene Maier

FLAGSHIP LINE

The Riviera series is typical of the company's continuous innovation. Conceived in 1973 as a large tuning-fork model, it had a unique 12-sided case; in 1975 it included several automatic models; in 1979 it went back to quartz in three sizes and by 1981 included a diver's model and World Timer. By its twentieth anniversary, there was a choice of three case finishes, mechanical or quartz movements, a chronograph, and a quartz Complication. By 1994 the series was responsible for 25 percent of the firm's production and 30 to 35 percent of its turnover.

The "PHI" symbol Φ was first used in 1964. It is a Greek letter that symbolizes the golden number, a theory of proportion and balance so perfect that Leonardo da Vinci named it "divine proportion" in 1509.

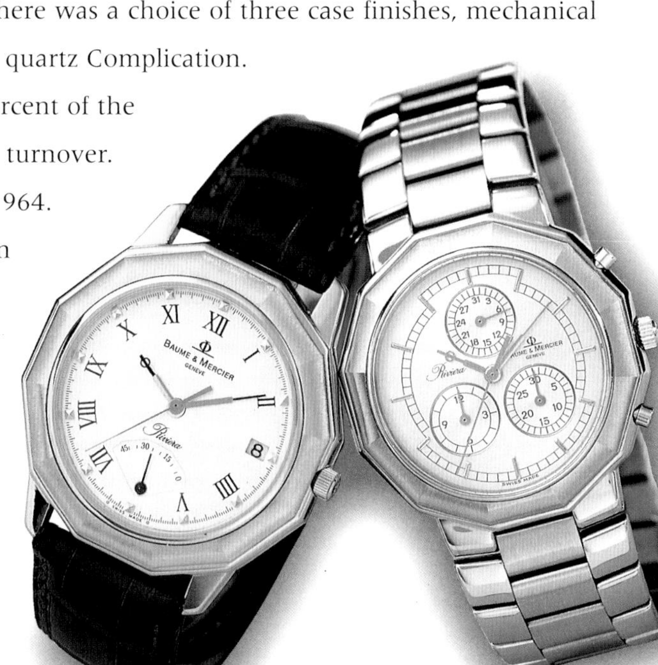

RIGHT
THE RIVIERA
Examples from the line, showing the unique 12-sided case.

№3

Bertolucci

Bertolucci's origins go back to 1967 and the arrival of Remo Bertolucci at a little workshop in Péry, near Bienne in the heart of the Swiss Jura, which had been the home of the Mimo watch company since 1911. The company had become known for its specialization in assembling watch movements.

The owner since 1936 had been Marcel Michelotti; Remo was his son-in-law. A native of Pisa and a qualified electroengineer, Bertolucci at first concentrated on purchasing and sales. Under his direction, the family business developed an important private label division. With exports initially destined for Portugal in 1969, they soon extended to Italy, Spain, Germany, France, and the United States and gave the business a truly international scope. After Bertolucci bought out his father-in-law in 1976, he set about creating his own brand. At the helm of his company and eager to create his own watch collection, he multiplied the company's projects. He gathered a young team of specialists with the aim of building manual and automatic watch movements by traditional methods, using the skills of artisan watchmakers. At the same time, he became familiar with the logistics of distribution. Having launched his first collection under his own name, he sold his first models in 1987.

In 1984 the company moved from Péry to Evilard, where mechanical movements were evolved and refined still more. Quartz movements were also developed here and in 1987 both kinds of movement found a new aesthetic guise with the presentation of the first collection of complete Bertolucci watches. In 1994 the firm moved to its present premises at Neuchâtel. The new workshop is an atelier equipped with the most modern technology, yet at the same time is architecturally beautiful, a combination of old and new entirely in keeping with the ancient and remarkable art of watchmaking.

ABOVE
JEWELRY
Diamond and emerald-encrusted jewelry watch with case and bracelet in 18kt gold.

ABOVE
LADIES
18kt gold case and bracelet, mother-of-pearl dial and self-winding movement.

RIGHT
PRETIOSA HIGH
Pink and white diamond-encrusted Pretiosa with case and bracelet in 18kt gold.

PRODUCT RANGE

Vir Gents and Ladies
Jewelry
Pretiosa High
Vir Chrono
Mini Vir

BERTOLUCCI

RIGHT
The Vir collection offers great variety. This jewel-encrusted model combines great beauty with practicality.

LEFT
Each link of the Vir bracelet is hand-polished to make it smooth and secure for utmost flexibility.

FACT FILE

FOUNDED: 1987
COUNTRY OF ORIGIN: Switzerland
OUTPUT: Information not available
MOVEMENT: Mechanical only
CEO: Remo Bertolucci

The Bertolucci collection consists principally of the Vir range of traditional models, including a certified Chronometer in a steel and gold case with a screwdown crown on a matching bracelet; a perpetual calendar in a similar large (38mm) case in 18-karat white gold with moonphases, also on a matching bracelet; and the Vir Diver's watch.

There is a Genus line in steel or gold cases on crocodile straps with handwound or automatic mechanical movements in a limited edition numbered from 1 to 100. The jewelry line includes a number of pieces set with meticulously cut diamonds, rubies, emeralds, and sapphires; the movements are 8¾ selfwinding Cal. 2000.

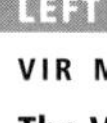

LEFT
VIR MARIS
The Vir collection combines all the qualities demanded by watches of great value and beauty.

FLAGSHIP LINE

The most popular design is the Vir Maris, a diver's watch with self-winding movement, in a huge (39.5mm) stainless steel case, water-resistant to 1000 feet with screwdown back and crown, and a curved sapphire crystal on a stainless steel bracelet.

BLANCPAIN

Blancpain marked its 260th anniversary with a special edition of its self-winding calendar watch with moonphase, limited to 260 pieces, offered in white or pink 18-karat gold.

Jehan-Jacques Blancpain's name first appeared on a watch in 1735. His factory was a large farmhouse in Villaret in the Vallée de Joux, and it was nearly 100 years before his great-grandson managed to build a small factory in which to make the complete watches which were beginning to acquire a reputation in France, Germany, and Russia. The business passed from father to son for thirteen generations until the death in 1932 of Frédéric-Emile Blancpain marked the end of the Blancpain dynasty. For the next forty years the firm was run by Madame Fichter, who had been one of Frédéric's closest colleagues; the name was changed to "Rayville" – an anagram of Villeret.

In the meantime, in 1926, the firm went into production with the world's first self-winding wristwatch, based on John Harwood's patented design. In 1953 a diver's watch water-resistant to a depth of 660 feet caused a stir when it was worn by Jacques Cousteau; it became standard issue to the French Navy. Then came the Ladybird, the most compact watch movement ever seen – a mere 5 lignes (11.85mm) in diameter.

PRODUCT RANGE

260th Anniversary
Flying Tourbillon
Chronograph
Ladies' automatic chronograph
2100 Series

JB 1735 BLANCPAIN

BELOW
BLANCPAIN
Gents ultra-thin watch in stainless steel on strap. Hand-wound mechanical movement. One of the six Masterpieces series.

LEFT
2100 SERIES
Gents steel watch, larger than average, with 100hr power reserve and automatic movement.

BELOW
2100 SERIES
Gents 18kt gold watch with leather strap featuring automatic "sports" date.

ABOVE

Ladies Chronograph – blending tradition and modernity and perfect for day or evening wear.

But the advent of quartz seriously affected the firm. It was taken over by a consortium of manufacturers including Omega, and the name Blancpain fell into disuse. Then in 1983, 250 years after its founding, the name Blancpain came back under its new owners.

Jean-Claude Biver, a former Managing Director of Omega, and Jacques Piguet, the son of the renowned ébauche manufacturer Frédéric Piguet, applied a wealth of experience and succeeded in restoring the name Blancpain to its former eminence.

In a farmhouse in Le Brassus in a building almost identical to the one in which the founder had worked, the new owners set up Blancpain's headquarters. They marked the occasion with the launch of an automatic wristwatch with perpetual calendar and phases of the moon – an innovation which they claim started the present fashion for moonphase watches. They also abandoned the idea of a collection; there would be just one case for men's watches and one for ladies, and every variation of movement would be built to fit them.

In a veritable *tour de force*, Blancpain produced in 1991 a series of six masterpieces of the watchmaker's art housed in identical cases and followed this with a single model which combined, incredibly, every distinguishing feature of each of the six watches.

ABOVE

The only Tourbillon with a power reserve of eight days – perfection in miniature.

LEFT

Chronograph with split seconds hand. The complexity, small diameter and extra-slim design of this movement make it into a work of art.

FACT FILE

FOUNDED: 1735
COUNTRY OF ORIGIN: Switzerland
OUTPUT: Information not available
MOVEMENT: Mechanical only
CEO: Jean-Claude Biver

Then, in 1994, came the 2100 series, designed to meet the demands of the 21st century. It was a self-winding calendar; 21 represents the new century and 100 indicates its 100-hour power reserve, its 100-hour test period, and its 100-meter – 330-foot – water-resistance; it gained the first prize in the "Swiss Watch of the Year" awards. As a tribute to the century's last leap year, the firm's watchmakers designed a timepiece which combined the complications of a chronograph with the complexities of a perpetual calendar. To round off the year, they created a minuscule lady's automatic for their Ladybird collection.

All Blancpain movements are mechanical; the company insists there has never been a quartz Blancpain and there never will be.

ABOVE
This latest creation from Blancpain is named after the lucky ladybird and is a triumph of elegant restraint.

FLAGSHIP LINE

As Blancpain still has no collection, it is difficult to pinpoint a flagship model, but the one which epitomizes their precision, complexity, and superb finish is probably the 2100.

LEFT
BLANCPAIN 2100

BREGUET

Another of the Great Houses whose factory is situated in the Vallée de Joux, Breguet comprises three companies: Montres Breguet, watchmakers since 1775; Nouvelle Lamania, a movement manufacturer; and Valdar, a specialist in micromechanical engineering.

RIGHT
CLASSIC
Gents ultra-slim watch in 18kt gold. Hand-wound movement.

Breguet's traditions were established by the founder Abraham-Louis Breguet, who is generally acknowledged to be the greatest watchmaker of all time. He is credited with having either invented or patented the majority of horological achievements, including, in 1780, the "perpetual" or automatic movement (in those days fitted into a pocket watch) the development of the perpetual date calendar; the Breguet balance spring; the tourbillon, whose balance and escapement are in a revolving cage; the parachut shock absorber; the double-barreled marine chronometer; and even the first wristwatch, made for the Queen of Naples in 1810. His clients included the rich and the famous, and his watches became the favorites of the Russian Court. The story goes that both Wellington and Napoleon consulted their Breguet watches during the Battle of Waterloo. Breguet – a Swiss who spent almost all his life in France – ran very much a one-man business. It was carried on after his death by a nephew, who formed a partnership with an Englishman, Edward Brown, who became the sole owner of the House of Breguet. But as often happens, the fortunes of the firm declined over the next century under a series of owners.

RIGHT
TYPE XX AERONAVALE
Single-action, instant-restart chronograph in polished-steel case and bracelet.

PRODUCT RANGE

Classic
Marine
Type XX Aeronavale

Breguet

RIGHT
MARINE
Gents Marine watch in 18kt gold and steel. The case is water-resistant to 150ft.

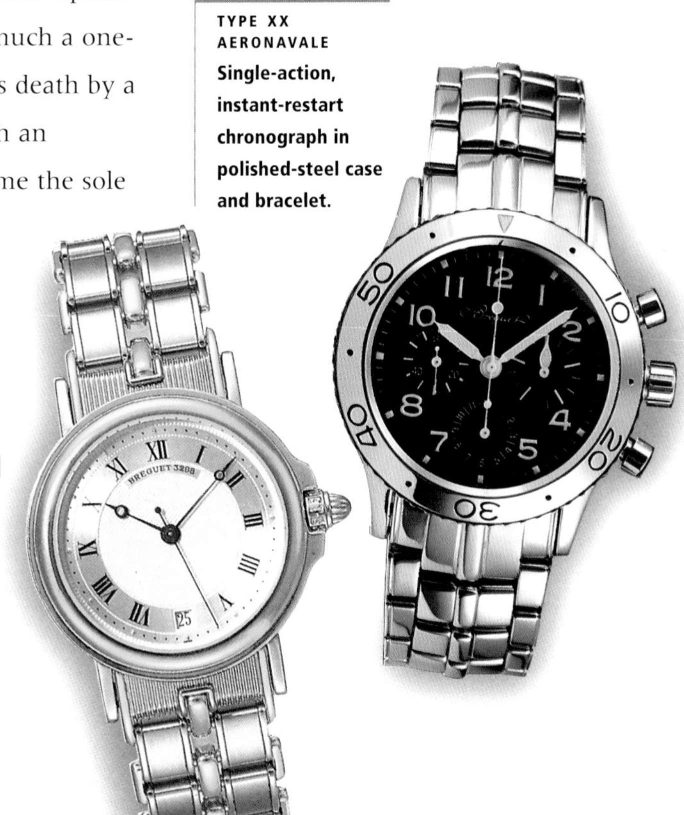

ABOVE
Louis Breguet (1880–1955) became one of the pioneers of aviation in 1907, following the spirit of his ancestors.

ABOVE
Invented in 1795 and patented in 1801, the tourbillon device remains the most familiar of Abraham-Louis Breguet's many inventions.

But the link was not lost. In the early 1900s, Abraham-Louis's great-great-grandson Louis was a pilot who built one of the first manned helicopters to actually lift off the ground. His company produced cockpit watches – the successors of which are still in use in commercial airlines today – but it did not make watches for the public.

Finally, after another dormant period, the brothers Chaumet, Parisian jewelers of note, bought the company in 1968 and set about restoring it to its former state; scarcely twenty years later, both companies were acquired by a wealthy international group with existing horological connections. Now, happily, the Breguet brand is in production once more in the Vallée de Joux.

ABOVE
This craftsman is bevelling an oscillating weight openworked into a "B".

The brand specializes in mechanical watches of considerable technical workmanship in finely wrought cases – often in small series. It has three product lines. Classic, a watch whose design is influenced by the example of the founder, is ultrathin, hand-wound or self-winding, chronographs or tourbillons, enriched by gemset models.

Marine is based on models supplied by A. L. Breguet to the French Navy. Water-resistant with sturdy cases and protected crowns, they have automatic movements and are offered in three sizes – men's, intermediate, and ladies.

Type XX Aeronavale: maintaining the connection with flying initiated by Louis Breguet in the early days of the century, this is a reissue of a model developed in the 1950s for the French Naval Air Service. An automatic chronograph, it has all the features of the original – black dial, tritium-coated hands and numerals, rotating bezel, and the famous *retour au vol* function, which at a single touch returns the chronograph to zero and restarts it immediately.

Of particular interest is Breguet's perpetual calendar and equation-of-time wristwatch, first patented in 1991. Now available in platinum, it has a hand-engraved movement visible through a sapphire caseback. It provides a perpetual indication of the difference between Real Solar Time and Mean Solar Time. The dial is typical of Abraham-Louis Breguet's layout.

RIGHT
One of the 500 numbered watches ordered by the French Naval Air Arm for its pilots in 1958.

FACT FILE

FOUNDED: 1775
COUNTRY OF ORIGIN: Switzerland/France
OUTPUT: Information not available
MOVEMENT: Mechanical only
CEO: Jean J. Jacober

FLAGSHIP LINE

The Marine series is the largest line in the range. It includes self-winding models with date and center seconds; 18-karat gold chronographs in gold and steel, some gemset in the smaller size; and a lady's "Marine" with automatic movements, center seconds and date, and water-resistant to 100 feet.

RIGHT
MARINE
Here in 18kt white gold, bezel and bracelet links encrusted with diamonds.

LEFT
The sophisticated movement in this Breguet pocket watch is there for all to see.

№6

Breitling

Louis Breitling opened a studio workshop in La Chaux de Fonds in 1884. In Germany Gottfried Daimler had patented his internal combustion engine, and Karl Benz had produced the first practical gasoline-driven automobile. Louis Breitling realized these new machines would need timing instruments and made it his aim to produce chronographs and timing devices for them.

ABOVE
CHRONOMAT
Limited Edition Red Arrows Chronomat, with striking red dial.

RIGHT
NAVITIMER
Navitimer Montbrillant, designed in the spirit of the 1940s, featuring the classic circular slide rule.

With the outbreak of war, his son Gaston devised a wrist chronometer for the artillery, while Louis's grandson Willy set his sights on higher things – the airplane. When Lindbergh navigated the *Spirit of St. Louis* across the Atlantic using a wristwatch, Willy saw the need for accurate cockpit timepieces. In 1936 he designed a dashboard chronograph which brought orders from some aircraft manufacturers for whom Breitling is still standard equipment.

It was a logical step from panel clocks to timekeepers, and in 1952 Breitling produced the model that became its international trademark – the Navitimer, the favorite of pilots all over the world. Ten years later, its supersonic version, the Cosmonaute, appeared. A chronograph with a 24-hour dial instead of the usual 12-hour one, it accompanied Scott Carpenter into space.

The aging Willy found it difficult to cope with the advent of quartz, and Ernest Schneider took over the company in 1979. He was no horologist, but an electronics engineer and a trained pilot; he was joined by another, François Thiebaud, and together they set up a new factory at Grenchen to meet the needs of the aircraft industry. They changed the movements to quartz and convinced their aeronautical clients that the new technique was reliable by introducing a unique

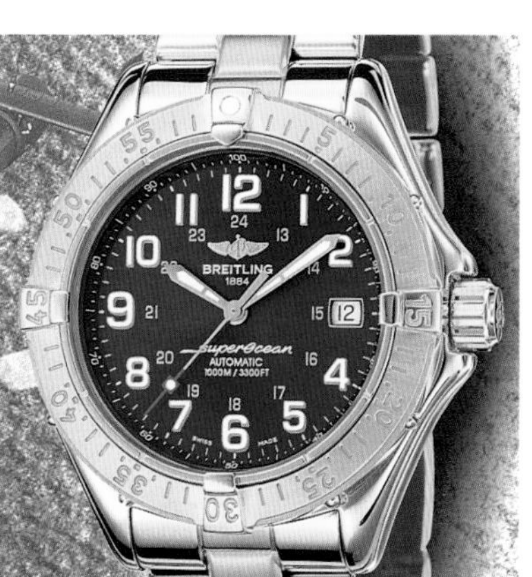

RIGHT
SUPEROCEAN
Colt Superocean, in 18kt gold, its case tough enough to withstand underwater pressures equivalent to 3,300ft.

PRODUCT RANGE

Chronomat
Navitimer
Montbrillant
Cosmonaute
Superocean
Scott Carpenter
Aerospace
Emergency

chronograph that displayed three time zones simultaneously and had two separate movements with independent power sources – a significant safety factor.

An encounter with Eric Tarbally, the famous yachtsman, led Schneider to develop a line of watches for yachtsmen; this was followed by a series of diver's models of increasing sophistication. For over a hundred years, Breitling has concentrated on producing what it calls "Instruments for Professionals." The product line includes the bestselling Chronomat; the Aerospace, originally designed for and used by the RAF Red Arrows and now available with a multifunction electronic movement with audible indication of hour and minute by pressing the crown (a world first); the Scott Carpenter, a handwound mechanical chronograph which is an identical replica of the one Commander Carpenter wore aboard the Aurora 7 space capsule; the Montbrillant, a high frequency self-winding chronograph which features the classic circular slide rule found on every Navitimer; and the Spatiographe, an especially complex automatic chronograph with a digital minute display system visible through a dial aperture that is especially appreciated by pilots.

RIGHT

Breitling Aerospace Repetition Minutes. Breitling continues to meet the needs of aviators.

ABOVE

"Blue Angels", another Breitling dedication to the men of the air.

FACT FILE

FOUNDED: 1884
COUNTRY OF ORIGIN: Switzerland
OUTPUT: Information not available
MOVEMENT: Mechanical and quartz Chronographs and timers
CEO: Ernest Schneider

The most recent example of Breitling's ingenuity is the Emergency – a wrist-worn instrument for pilots that, in addition to its chronometric functions, incorporates a minuscule transistor which, in the event of an accident, can send a signal on the international distress frequency to assist rescuers.

BELOW

BREITLING CHRONOMAT

FLAGSHIP LINE

The Breitling Chronomat, a leader in the field of mechanical chronographs, has been improved and modified in the ten years since its launch. It is water-resistant to 330 feet, has a unidirectional turning bezel, and sapphire glareproof crystal. Available in steel, steel and gold, or solid 18-karat gold on leather strap or matching bracelet.

BULGARI

It all began when a Greek silversmith left his native village of Epirus in 1879 and emigrated to Italy. There, five years later Sotirio Bulgari opened his first shop in Rome; in 1905, with his two sons Constantino and Giorgio, he moved to the Via Condotti, still the flagship of Bulgari shops today.

ABOVE
SPORTS LINE
18 kt gold Sport, water-resistant with automatic movement.

In the first decades of the 20th century, the two brothers laid the foundations of a flourishing jewelry business. By the 1970s the firm of Bulgari had become an international jeweler supported by its own 44 shops, including those in New York, Paris, Monte Carlo, and Geneva.

Although the firm had been selling watches since the 1920s using movements from the top Swiss manufacturers like Audemars Piguet, Jaeger-LeCoultre, and Vacheron Constantin, it was not until 1977 that the firm launched its own first important collection. It was so successful that, three years later, Bulgari Time was founded in Neuchâtel, Switzerland, to manage the creation and production of Bulgari watches.

To make sure the quality of the inside workings matched that of the Bulgari cases, the firm signed a joint venture with Girard Perregaux in 1989 for the production of the movements.

An early example of a Bulgari watch is the gold pocket watch made in the 1930s. Fitted with an Audemars Piguet movement, it was bought by Count Galazzo Ciano as a gift to celebrate a friend's appointment as Italian ambassador to Turkey. Ottavio de Peppo had served in the Italian Foreign Ministry under Ciano for four years – a period engraved on the back, the Roman figures XII to XVI marking the twelfth to sixteenth year of the Fascist era.

PRODUCT RANGE

Antiteatro
Bulgari-Bulgari
Quadrato
Parentesi
Alveare
Antalia
Sports Line
Chronograph
Tourbillon
Trika
Minute Repeater

BVLGARI

LEFT
QUADRATO
Stainless steel Quadrato, water-resistant, with quartz movement.

RIGHT
TRIKA
18kt gold Trika with diamond dial and gold bracelet.

FACT FILE

FOUNDED: 1884
COUNTRY OF ORIGIN: Italy
OUTPUT: Information not available
MOVEMENT: Mechanical 30%, quartz 70%
CEO: Francesco Trapani

Another fabulous creation was a bracelet watch designed as a serpent. Created in the late 1940s, its supple and flexible body is of polished yellow gold. The movement, by Movado, is concealed in the jeweled head. In the 1970s the snake wristwatch became more stylized, consisting of plain flexible spirals devoid of head or tail, and became a central theme of Bulgari's work at this time.

There are six different collections in the current Bulgari line. Most popular is Bulgari-Bulgari, a classic round model in two sizes with the Bulgari name engraved twice on the bezel. The watches have Swiss quartz or mechanical automatic movements, the cases are 18-karat gold or stainless steel and fitted with saddle leather straps or matching bracelets; some have diamond-set dials. The Antiteatro line takes its name from the concave design of the case between crystal and dial. There are two sizes, in 18-karat yellow or white gold, some with diamond-set bezels; they have quartz movements.

ABOVE **The mark of quality – the Bulgari name imprinted on Minute Repeater movement.**

One of Bulgari's latest designs is the Quadrato, a square watch in 18-karat gold set with diamonds, sapphires, rubies, and emeralds on matching gold bracelets. They have Swiss quartz movements. Men's models are available in plain 18-karat gold or stainless steel. Parentesi, Alveare, and Antalia are small collections of ladies integral bracelet models in 18-karat gold, some with diamond-set dials.

In the Sports Line, which has Swiss automatic mechanical movements in gold or stainless steel cases on a strap or bracelet, are a selection of scuba diver's watches with certified chronometer movements and water-resistance to 660 feet. There is also a line of Quartz Chronometers.

Bulgari also offers a pair of Grande Complications. A Minute Repeater, which marks the hours, quarters, and minutes, and has a sapphire caseback to reveal the movement, is available in 18-karat gold or platinum; a Tourbillon model has an open-work dial in an 18-karat case with gold hands and numerals on a silver dial.

FLAGSHIP LINE

Bulgari's star performer is Bulgari-Bulgari. First produced in 1977, the original version has a gold case and leather strap and is now considered a classic. Like Quadrato, Bulgari-Bulgari is also available on the famous Tubogas Wraparound snake bracelet.

BELOW **BULGARI-BULGARI With Tubogas bracelet.**

Cartier

The name Cartier has been synonymous with luxury goods since Louis-François Cartier took over the workshop of master jeweler Adolphe Picard in Paris in 1847. Cartier was a jeweler first and a watchmaker second. His dazzling creations were bought by the rich and famous in the courts of Europe for their beauty – their timekeeping was secondary. But in 1904, a friend, Alberto Santos-Dumont, asked him to make an accurate timepiece to check the performance of his airship. Louis Cartier got together with a Swiss friend named LeCoultre to design one especially for him; it was Cartier's first wristwatch, and it opened up a new chapter in the firm's history.

PRODUCT RANGE

Tank
Pasha
Baignoire
Pasha Golf
Louis Cartier Tourbillon
Santos
Must de Cartier

Cartier

Louis Cartier put the Santos-Dumont watch into production. He introduced a *tonneau* model (named after the type of barrel in which the French store wine); then in 1917, inspired, as he said, by the stark outline of the Allied war machines lumbering across the battlefields of Flanders, he invented the "Tank" design, which Cartier has made spectacularly its own. Many famous people became his clients, and he opened branches of the firm in their favorite watering holes – St. Moritz, Monte Carlo, and Nice. Later the firm expanded into London's Bond Street and New York's Fifth Avenue. He bought his movements from the best Swiss houses and cased them up in a Paris factory built especially for the purpose in 1950.

In 1965 the last of the family interests was sold, and the famous name might have died out but for a group of investors led by a Swiss businessman, Joseph Kanoui, who over the next 15 years took over all the Cartier interests around the world.

LEFT
MUST DE CARTIER
Colisée Vermeil with ivory dial and ardillon strap.

LEFT
BAIGNOIRE
18kt gold case with diamonds, crocodile strap. The Grand Duchess Maria Pavlovna, for whom the watch was originally designed in 1912, associated the graceful oval case with her bathtub, hence the name.

ABOVE
PANTHER
Steel and gold case and bracelet. Water-resistant to 100ft, quartz movement.

In 1981 the consortium formed Cartier International and put one of their young executives – Alain Dominique Perrin – in charge; he is still its president today.

Perrin instigated a dynamic program of research and development, especially new materials and techniques, in both quartz and mechanical production. Old established watchmakers Baume et Mercier and Piaget were acquired, along with several associated companies, and a new factory at Villaret was set up in conjunction with Ebel to produce the group's timepieces.

The first model to result from all this was the Pasha, a modern version of a watch originally made by Cartier for the ruler of Marrakesh, who wanted a watch he could swim in. It is still one of Cartier's most popular models. The line encompasses both quartz and mechanical movements and includes such collections as the Panthère, in solid gold or with pavé diamonds; the Pasha Golf, a complex gemset model that can record four golf scores in windows on its silvered dial; or the Baignoire, in a graceful oval case decorated with diamonds and pearls in a stylized garland of leaves.

ABOVE
Examples from the Pasha line, innovative watches with a modern, sporty design.

RIGHT
21 Must de Cartier – a youthful, dynamic range 20 years ahead of its time. In polished, brushed steel, they can be worn with leather strap or steel bracelet.

RIGHT
Pocket watch with mechanical movement, red and black enamel patterned back and silvered crystal and lacquer dial.

FACT FILE

FOUNDED: 1847
COUNTRY OF ORIGIN: France
OUTPUT: Information not available
MOVEMENT: Mechanical and quartz
CEO: Alain Dominique Perrin

LEFT
Pasha de Cartier – a decidedly elegant and masculine model. The round casing, with dial in white, grey or navy, creates a harmonious simplicity.

ABOVE
American Tank Chronoreflex, in yellow gold with 3 rows of full-cut diamonds and full-cut alligator bracelet. The dial is of stippled silver.

FLAGSHIP LINE

The Tank remains Cartier's most memorable design and includes eleven different versions – Chinois, Americaine, Allongé, etc. In 1996 Cartier designed the Tank Française, a square model with a slightly curved gold case with an integrated bracelet and the familiar black Roman numerals protected by a sapphire crystal; the unusual winder has a sapphire cabochon.

ABOVE
THE TANK

№9

Chaumet

Established in Paris in 1780, Chaumet has a long tradition of creating fine jewelry for the courts of Europe since the time of Emperor Napoleon I, when the firm's founder Maire-Etienne Nitot was appointed court jeweler to the Empire in 1804. Nitot, as well as creating fabulous pieces of jewelry, also made watches set with precious stones which were often given as mementos to diplomats and friends of the court.

In 1848 a partner in the firm named Morel opened a shop in London and Queen Victoria became one of his clients; his daughter married a talented young jeweler named Joseph Chaumet, who subsequently received several commissions from the Maharajahs of India and in 1908 received the Royal Warrant from King Edward VII.

In the late 1960s, the then Chaumet Brothers tried to re-establish the renowned Breguet brand, but they were overtaken by events and became part of the international group Investcorp, who already had horological interests in Nouvelle Lamania and Gucci. Pierre Haquet, a former Managing Director (CEO) of Cartier International, was given the task of reviving the company's fortunes.

Among Chaumet's collections are the Anneau line of watches with quartz movements in silver or gold round cases which have a series of interchangeable bracelets in alligator, lambskin, pearls, satin, or gold, and with diamonds if desired.

There is a jumping-hour model called Les Pleiades, which has a self-winding mechanical movement whose gleaming polished case features two windows. These windows display the hours (in the upper) and minutes (in the lower). The hour, as the name implies, jumps forward every 60 minutes.

RIGHT
AQUILA I
Gents 18kt gold and steel case with matching bracelet, champagne quillochet dial, gold Roman figures and hands, sapphire crystal, quartz movement.

ABOVE
ANNEAU
18kt gold watch. The bracelets in this exclusive series are interchangeable.

RIGHT
ANNEAU
Gold square watch, one of a varied collection, with black lizard strap.

PRODUCT RANGE

Khésis
Anneau
Aquila
Les Pleiades
Style de Chaumet
Man's minute repeater
Man's chronograph

CHAUMET

ABOVE
Design for a watch for the Duchesse de Luynes, approved by her husband and returned to Morel in October 1853.

ABOVE
Watches from the "Khésis" Collection. Shown here are "Classic Lady" and "Top Lady," with steel case and bracelet. The movement is quartz.

Aquila II is a masculine-size line of quartz watches with day/date and a slim brushed-steel case which the company hopes women will also find attractive. It comes with a leather strap or integrated bracelet. The latest collection of timepieces, named "Style de Chaumet," consists of a line of 30 models, offered in gold or steel, in large or small models, with quartz or automatic movements. In addition, there is the existing Khésis collection of ladies watches in steel or gold square cases with a slightly curved profile, all with quartz movements.

In its collection Chaumet also has a minute repeater and a chronograph, each in an 18-karat gold case on a strap with a mechanical movement.

FACT FILE

FOUNDED: 1780
COUNTRY OF ORIGIN: France
OUTPUT: Information not available
MOVEMENT: Mechanical and quartz
CEO: Pierre Haquet

FLAGSHIP LINE

The Khésis collection for women takes its name from the Navajo word for the sun, the emblem of the Place Vendôme in Paris, home to the House of Chaumet. The line includes 32 variations on a theme, from an all-steel modern watch to a most unusual steel model set with diamonds to a sophisticated gold-cased version set with pavé diamonds. All Khésis watches have square cases with a curved profile and choice of dials and have quartz movements.

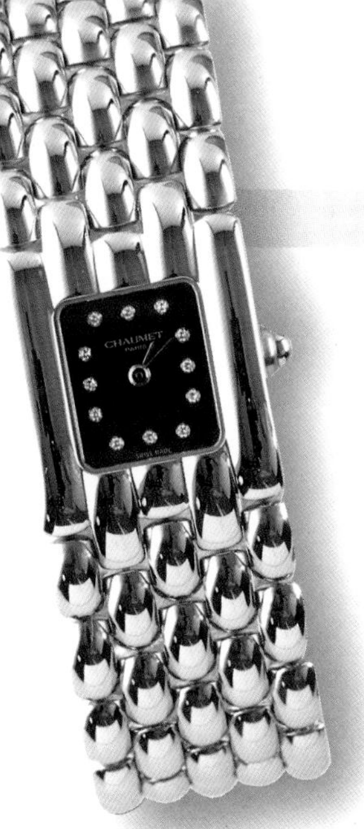

RIGHT
KHESIS
Stainless steel, black face, with diamonds index.

Chopard

In 1860 Louis-Ulysse Chopard set up a small factory in Sonvillier in the Swiss Jura to make pocket watches – which were particularly favored by railroad employees for their reliability. Later his son branched out into jewelry watches, and his success brought about a move in 1920 to the then urban center of the horological world – Geneva.

PRODUCT RANGE

Classic
Casmir
Gstaad
Happy Diamonds
Happy Sport
St. Moritz

Chopard

One hundred years after it began, the company was in the aging hands of Paul André-Chopard, grandson of the founder, whose two sons showed no desire to enter the declining business. Rescue came out of the blue from Germany.

At the turn of the century, a family named Scheufele had established a factory in the jewelry center of Pforzheim. They built up a flourishing business making jewelry and watches, bracelets, and cases. In World War II, Pforzheim was almost totally destroyed, and the Scheufele family had to build up their business once again. By 1963, the firm was again prosperous and looking for work to put in a newly built factory at Birkenfeld. They had always used Swiss movements in their watches, and when they decided to try to acquire a Swiss watchmaking house, they chanced upon Chopard.

Under Karl Scheufele – the third generation of Karls – production was rationalized, using Pforzheim for making jewelry and cases, and Geneva for building and assembling the

LEFT
IMPERIALE
Chronograph in 18kt gold, encrusted with diamonds and rubies.

RIGHT
HAPPY SPORT
Ladies watch in 18kt white gold, set with diamonds and sapphires. Water-resistant to 100ft.

LEFT
GSTAAD
Ladies watch in 18kt gold, set with diamonds. Water-resistant to 100ft.

watches. Output rose to more than 30,000 watches a year, with 15,000 pieces of jewelry from the Birkenfeld factory, which specialized in diamond setting. Soon the distinctive blend of high fashion and fine watchmaking which had become the hallmark of Chopard was being recognized in over 50 countries.

Chopard has remained a family business. At its head, Karl controls the Swiss operation; his wife Karin looks after Birkenfeld and the jewelry; and son Karl-Frederich oversees mechanical production, while daughter Caroline's creative flair is responsible for their imaginative jewelry and jeweled watches.

FACT FILE

FOUNDED: 1860
COUNTRY OF ORIGIN: Switzerland
OUTPUT: 30,000 plus per annum
MOVEMENT: 35% mechanical, 65% quartz
High fashion jewelry watches
CEO: Karl Scheufele

ABOVE
Happy Sport comes in so many variations, dressed in diamonds and decorated with sapphires, rubies or emeralds.

There are a number of clearly defined collections in the product range. The more masculine designs are in the Mille Miglia line of quartz watches in steel or 18-karat gold. A recent innovation is a chronograph with water-resistance to 330 feet. The St. Moritz models have a more sporting aspect, with their unusual bezels held down by screws; the men's models have automatic movements, the ladies' are quartz with bezels inset with diamonds.

The Casmir collection is Caroline's special creation. Based on the centuries-old paisley motif, the piece is woven into an extravaganza of gold and precious stones. In the Classical collection, the men's perpetual calendar chronograph (which employs the exclusive Jaeger-LeCoultre 889 movement – a rare privilege), was released last year in a limited edition of 150 pieces in gold.

But the flagship of Chopard's horological jewelry is their "Happy Diamonds" concept, in which seven diamonds edged with gold float freely around the dial between two plates of scratchproof sapphire crystal. A subsequent development is the "Happy Sport" collection, designed to be worn all day as a sporty alternative to the more precious jewelry watches.

BELOW
HAPPY DIAMONDS

FLAGSHIP LINE

The "Happy Diamonds" line, with its seven diamonds freely floating above the dial, is available in 18-karat gold cases embellished in a variety of styles with diamond and sapphires. The movements are quartz; the watches are water-resistant to 100 feet.

Nº11

Christian Dior

Christian Dior, having created with Marcel Boussac the "New Look" which revolutionized the fashion world, opened his own fashion house in 1947 and immediately set about diversifying into fashion accessories, perfume, and jewelry; in 1970 he introduced his first collection of watches. In 1975 he launched the first Christian Dior watch and for five years concentrated on classical shapes – square, rectangular – and classic materials, solid gold or stainless steel, with mechanical or automatic movements.

ABOVE

JUBILE

A Dior classic, its rectangular gadrooned case reminiscent of the thirties.

In 1980 he introduced a line of gold-plated models, with varying dial colors and hexagonal cases, all on straps. Then came the introduction of metal bracelets and the use of gadroons in general. 1985 saw the Black Moon, described as the "New Look" for watches, followed by Swing – in octagonal cases in ten-micron gold-plate on straps or bracelets, and Jubilé to mark the 40th anniversary of the House of Dior, in gold-plated rectangular cases reminiscent of the 30s.

Success is a line of round gadrooned cases in two sizes, and Baghera is a gold-plated version of the Black Moon, its black dial relieved only by gilt hands and the Dior logo. In the early 90s Dior moved upscale with the Heure Sublime collection in steel or 18-karat gold cases with modern linked bracelets. Ultrathin batons on the dial, with its date window at 4 o'clock, give a very modern appearance. More intricate models, with dials, bezels, and bracelets set with Top Wesselton diamonds, put this collection into the luxury class.

Then Dior created what has become his most popular line – La Parisienne – chunky square gold-plated or steel cases with a unique system of interchangeable straps or

PRODUCT RANGE

Heure Sublime
Swing
La Parisienne
Rialto
Jubilé
Monsieur Dior

ChristianDior

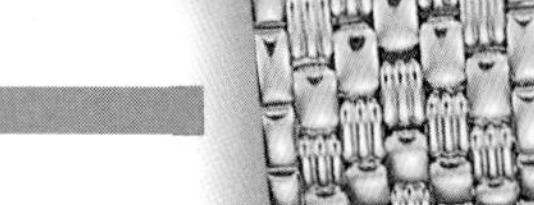

RIGHT

RIALTO

Gold plated, with octagonal case, sapphire glass and supple bracelet.

BELOW

HEURE SUBLIME

In steel and 18kt gold. The round case has a slightly curved profile.

ABOVE
Parisienne watches come in a variety of guises, all of them elegant.

bracelets. The steel version has a houndstooth strap, while the gold-plated model has a choice of 20 watch bands in silk, lizard, or calf, or gold-plated bracelets with clip-on decoration in citrine colors – an exclusive Dior idea and a very feminine collection for ladies only. For men there is Monsieur Dior – a similar square case but with distinctive beveled bezel in steel or gold plate on a strap or finely chiseled metal bracelet.

All Christian Dior watches have high-quality Swiss quartz movements and are water-resistant to 100 feet. The watches are assembled in Switzerland. The first couturier to produce a watch branded with his name, Dior is adamant that his watches are a major product, not just a fashion accessory.

ABOVE
An expression of French elegance and luxury – Parisienne in presentation box.

FACT FILE

FOUNDED: 1975
COUNTRY OF ORIGIN: France (Swiss watches)
OUTPUT: Information not available
MOVEMENT: Quartz
CEO: Philippe Mougenot

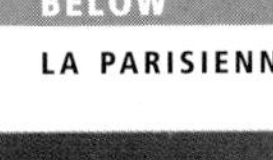

BELOW
LA PARISIENNE

FLAGSHIP LINE

La Parisienne, in steel- or gold-plated cases with a distinctive canework motif reminiscent of the chairs at a Paris fashion show. The special feature is the interchangeability of straps or bracelet, thanks to a unique system. There are 20 different strap or bracelet versions, including moiré silk and houndstooth. A further variation is possible by clipping citrine decorations onto the bracelet. There is even a travel case for holding a variety of watch bands.

№12

Chronoswiss

Chronoswiss is the concept of Gerd R. Lang, a German watchmaker who in 1981 set out to manufacture high-quality exclusively mechanical wristwatches – against the prevailing trend for quartz models.

ABOVE
KLASSIK
The Klassik Chronograph, with analog date register, 12 hour registers, tachymeter scale and applied hour markers.

Lang was convinced there was a market among collectors and connoisseurs for limited editions of high-quality mechanical watches, based on well-known Swiss calibers and hand-finished to precise standards in his own workshops. The designs would be traditional, but production would make use of the latest technology. He called his company Chronoswiss because, although it would be based in Munich, he intended his chronographs to have only the best Swiss movements.

Lang was born in Hanover and spent his early life working as a watchmaker in Germany before moving to Switzerland. There he worked for Heuer for ten years, learning a great deal about split-second timing and writing a definitive work on chronographs. He set up his own business in the late 1970s.

ABOVE
REGULATEUR
18kt gold/stainless steel case, water-resistant to 100ft, with screw-on strap attachments.

Lang's first watch was produced in 1982; it was a chronograph with date and moonphase. Production was limited by the small number of movements he could acquire, but all his first models were bought and are now collectors' pieces or in museums.

There are several lines in the Chronoswiss collection. Kairos uses the ETA 2892 self-winding movement with the date at 6 o'clock. It is available in three sizes of case, including a ladies model water-resistant to 100 feet, which is very popular. A chronograph version, based on the Valjou 7750 ébauche, was included later. Klassik is another line, also based on the Valjou movement, with cases of stainless steel or 18-karat pink gold, while Cabrio is a collection of

LEFT
OREA
With handmade baked enamel dial, blue steel hands and scratchproof sapphire crystal.

PRODUCT RANGE

Chronograph
Rattrapante
Regulateur
Klassik
Kairos
Cabiro
Orea
Lunar
Opus

ABOVE
Assembly. The demand for Chrono Swiss watches is so great that the 15 staff of this small company find it hard to keep up with production.

rectangular models in which, at the touch of a button at 6 o'clock, the center flips over to reveal the back of the decorated automatic movement, protected by scratchproof sapphire crystal. The Pacific 100 line is a particularly water-protected series in steel cases with screwdown crowns. As usual, there is a Chronograph version with the customary stopwatch and elapsed time counters.

Orea models are equipped with genuine enamel dials, a rarity even among the better watches these days, and have the extra-flat hand-wound ETA 7001 movement.

The Chronoswiss collection includes an automatic chronograph Rattrapante – i.e. with split seconds – and a certified chronometer in a choice of case materials but Lang's finest creation is possibly his Chronograph–Chronometer with an official chronometer certificate.

One of the distinguishing features of Chronoswiss watches is the milled edge on the bezel and the intricate guillochet work on the majority of the silver dials.

RIGHT
Cabrio – the watch with two faces. The back of this watch can be revealed without it having to leave the wrist.

FACT FILE

FOUNDED: 1983
COUNTRY OF ORIGIN: Germany
OUTPUT: 15,000 pieces per annum
MOVEMENT: Mechanical only
CEO: Gerd R. Lang

FLAGSHIP LINE

Chronoswiss has no real flagship model since its production is so small and each model is made in very limited quantities. The Kairos collection is the most popular; Chronograph is a watch of precision and character, and Opus was voted Watch of the Year in 1996 in Germany.

LEFT
KAIROS CHRONOGRAPH

№13

CITIZEN

Citizen, the world's largest watchmaker with around 21 percent of global production, was founded in 1930. In its brief history it has produced a significant number of top technical products; among its highlights are the world's flattest watch, and the world's smallest quartz movement, a professional diver's watch (Citizen Hyper Aqualand) capable of communicating with a PC.

ABOVE
ECO-DRIVE TITANIUM
Titanium watch, with allergy-resistant titanium case.

Of more use to ordinary mortals is the quartz Eco-Drive, powered by light which passes through dials made from ceramic or a special plastic and falls onto a photoelectric cell that converts it into electrical energy. This energy is then stored until it is required. The watch has all the accuracy of quartz, without a battery. One minute of bright sunlight to one hour of office lighting will keep it going for a whole day; fully charged it will last from 2 to 6 months (depending on the model) without further exposure to light.

ABOVE
ECO-DRIVE SLIM
This quartz watch is barely three-sixteenths-of-an-inch in cross-section.

The Eco-Drive comes in a choice of traditional men's designs in steel on strap or bracelet or in lightweight titanium, fashioned from a single block and water-resistant to 330 feet. There is a chunky sports model with luminous hands and batons, and a chronograph accurate to 1/20th second with split times which also features an alarm. A lady's Eco-Drive was also launched this year.

Even more technically impressive is the Eco-Drive Radio Controlled model. It receives signals from one of the universally coordinated (UCT) time stations around the world, which keeps the watch incredibly accurate. The latest model in the series is the EcoDrive Slim, housed in a nickel-free steel case with gilt embellishments on a matching two-tone bracelet.

The supreme example of Citizen's

PRODUCT RANGE

Eco-Drive
Eco-Drive Slim
Eco-Drive Ladies
Eco-Drive Titanium
Eco-Drive Radio Controlled
Promaster Aqualand
Promaster Navisurf

CITIZEN

RIGHT
PROMASTER NAVISURF
Offers the world's time zones at a glance, and employs the latest analog/digital display technology.

innovative technology is probably the Space Master Chronograph – the world's first radio-controlled watch with chronograph functions in analog display. It sets itself once a day, switches automatically from summer to winter time, it has self-illuminating numbers and hands, a stopwatch accurate to 1/20th secs, a tachymeter, and an alarm. The hi-tech antenna is incorporated in the casing.

ABOVE
Tanashi Factory, Tokyo, Japan. Citizen is the world's largest watch producer.

The Citizen Promaster Aqualand is another marvel of technology with its sensitive microelectronic depth measurement and special diving functions – a watch and diving computer in one. It stores dive time, maximum diving depth, lowest water temperature, date, and start and end of dives for the previous four dives. The data is read on two digital displays. What's more, during a dive the present diving depth is indicated, and at the press of a button, dive time, maximum diving depth achieved, and water temperature can be called up. Depth is measured between 4 feet and 260 feet at one-foot intervals, and dive time up to 100 minutes. It even has a diving depth alarm which sounds as soon as maximum depth has been exceeded – it also warns if ascending speed is too rapid.

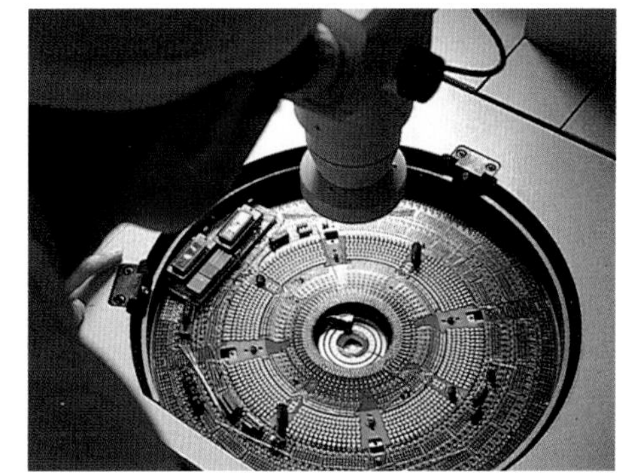

ABOVE
The LSI test system. Citizen is the company most often associated with the leading edge of consumer-driven technology.

The Navisurf combines display of the world's time zones at a glance with two different timers for yacht racing. It displays Greenwich Mean Time (UTC) on one analog dial, local time on the main analog dial, and a third time zone with designated city on the digital display. It also has two alarms and has 330 feet of water resistance.

BELOW
ECO-DRIVE
Radio-controlled, at the top of Citizen's flagship line.

FLAGSHIP LINE

The Eco-Drive with its variety of models – traditional, sports, chronograph, and slim version, with the Radio Controlled model at the top of the pyramid, is undoubtedly Citizen's flagship line. Chronographs now represent the largest section of Citizen's sales.

FACT FILE

FOUNDED: 1930
COUNTRY OF ORIGIN: Japan
OUTPUT: 228 million units
MOVEMENT: Quartz
CEO: Mr. Tadayuki Sakakibara

№14

CORUM

In 1955 Gaston Reis, a talented watchmaker, took his nephew René Bannwart into partnership in the small watch factory which he had founded in La Chaux de Fonds in 1924. Bannwart brought with him the experience of twenty years in two of Geneva's most prestigious watch factories: they invented the name Corum and devised a logo – "the key to perfect time."

ABOVE

TRES RICHES HEURES

This 18kt gold watch is encrusted with 377 diamonds.

ABOVE

COIN WATCH

A 20 dollar gold coin converted into a precious quartz watch.

The firm soon acquired a reputation, not only for the high quality of its watches, but for the originality of its designs. Examples include the Golden Tube, the Chinese Hat, the Longchamp with its concealed lugs. These are all now collector's pieces. Then the firm's craftsmen brought out the Coin watch, choosing for their first models the American "Double Eagle" which, sliced in two, contained an ultrathin mechanical movement; later they introduced other smaller coins for ladies, using a quartz movement. Corum even designed a watch fashioned from a golden ingot, framed in an 18-karat gold case containing the slimmest of movements, which could be worn on the wrist or as a pendant. A platinum version was produced in 1978.

A glance at Corum's current catalog reveals a host of gemset creations, of perpetual calendars housed in precious cases, of bracelet watches – the Romulus series – with Roman numerals engraved or set with diamonds on the bezel. One outstanding technical achievement is the Golden Bridge, in which the minuscule 18-karat gold parts of the movement with its straight-line gear train are suspended in a clear sapphire crystal.

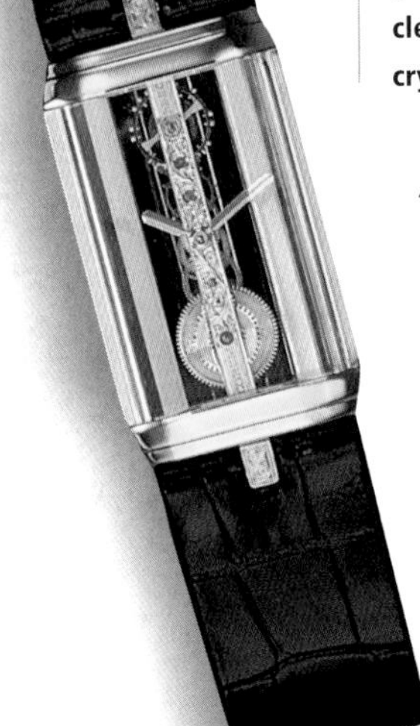

LEFT

GOLDEN BRIDGE

The 18kt gold mechanism is suspended like a golden bridge in a clear sapphire crystal.

But Corum's most famous collection is the "Admiral's Cup." The basis of the design is a 12-sided case corresponding to the 12 hours. The hour markers are pennants, indicating the numbers 1 – 12 in the International Maritime Code. It is available in solid gold, gold and steel, gold and blue steel, or all-steel water-resistant cases and can be found with an automatic or quartz movement.

PRODUCT RANGE

Admiral's Cup
Coin Watch
Golden Bridge
Ingot Watch
Romulus
Argos
Limelight
Très Riches Heures

Variations in the Admiral's Cup series include the "Fastnet" model, a chronograph version with automatic mechanical or quartz movement with seven functions; and "Marées," a unique and patented automatic movement which gives tidal information such as height, high or low strength of current, and time next full tide, as well as date and moonphase. "Régaté" has an electronic countdown system connected to its automatic movement, operated by a push button at 2 o'clock, which monitors the last vital ten minutes before the start of the race.

Other models in Corum's selection of over 400 different designs include a slim automatic with two mainspring barrels and a power reserve of 100 hours, and Tabagon, which at the touch of a button transforms into a small clock. It is available with quartz or mechanical movement with manual wind, in steel or 18-karat yellow, pink, or white gold. For the ladies there is the Arcus line of oval-cased watches, decorated with a mixture of diamonds and rubies, even on the hour markers, and with quartz movements.

The company no longer makes all its own movements, preferring to select the best examples of other famous houses such as Piaget and Jaeger-LeCoultre, but all Corum watches, whether quartz or mechanical, are finished in-house by Corum's own master craftsmen.

BELOW
In 1991 Corum called for tenders from newly qualified architects in Switzerland and four years later their new premises, as innovative as Corum's products, were inaugurated.

ABOVE
The engraver's tool outlines the hours in gold using Roman numerals, adding an original touch to the classical beauty of ultraflat "Romulus".

FACT FILE

FOUNDED: 1955
COUNTRY OF ORIGIN: Switzerland
OUTPUT: 18,000 per annum
MOVEMENT: Mechanical 60%, quartz 40%
CEO: Jean Réné Bannwart

FLAGSHIP LINE

"Admiral's Cup" with its 12-sided case and dial showing the numbers 1 – 12 as pennants of the International Maritime Code, a registered trademark of the company. It was named after the famous biannual race off the south coast of England, of which Corum is one of the sponsors. It has a number of variations – Fastnet, Marées, Régaté, Winner. Registered in 1983, Admiral's Cup is typical of the spirit of Corum's creativity.

RIGHT
ADMIRAL'S CUP

№15

George Daniels

Dr. George Daniels MBE, FAS, FBHI (an Honorary Doctorate of Science was conferred on him by London's City University in May 1994) is Britain's (some would say the world's) greatest living horologist and is the only Englishman in the last 300 years to have made virtually every part of a watch, including cases, hands, and engine-turned dials, with his own two hands. Not once, but many times – at the rate of one every year for the last 25 years.

ABOVE
Four-minute Tourbillon wristwatch with subsiding chronograph and coaxial escapement. 18kt gold case and silver dial.

George Daniels was drafted into the British army in 1944, and when he left the service in 1947 he spent his £50 gratuity on the best tools he could afford and got a job as a watch repairer. He soon realized that there was a big gap between his amateur status and that of the professionals. He enrolled in evening classes where he studied under E. H. Harrison; at the end of the three-year course, he took the Skinner Prize for the best work and was awarded an immediate Fellowship of the British Horological Institute.

Gradually he built up a reputation as a first-class repairer to the trade, and the financial rewards enabled him to indulge his other passion – for vintage Bentleys.

After three years, by which time he had worked up a useful connection with a number of dealers in antique watches, he met Cecil Clutton, a well-known collector. Clutton introduced George to the works of some of England's famous watchmakers, also to Breguet's. George was fascinated by the craftsmanship of these early masters and in particular found himself *en rapport* with the attitude of Breguet, so different from the others.

ABOVE
Reverse of same watch showing tourbillon. Every part was made in Daniels' own workshop.

For the next ten years, he devoted himself to the restoration of antique watches, concentrating particularly on those made by Breguet, of which he repaired nearly 400. He did his own drawings, took hundreds of photographs, and became the world's acknowledged expert on the master-watchmaker.

As a tribute to the master, he wrote the definitive work, *The Art of Breguet* (which although written in 1969 was not published until 1975) and then set about making his own first watch. At a time when the rest of the world was turning toward the new electronic technology, Daniels started a one-man mechanical renaissance. He had just turned 40.

From the start he knew what his watch should look like; the diameter, the position of the parts, and the layout of the dial were already firmly placed in his mind – even the design of what has become his traditional pendant and bow. It took two years to make, and he sold it to Clutton for £2,000. (Five years later he bought it back for £8,000!)

This was the beginning of George Daniels' most creative phase. He recognized early that the escapement invented by Thomas Mudge in 1754 had a major problem which impeded progress toward improved timekeeping – friction between the parts. He set out to design the seemingly impossible – a mechanical escapement that would not require lubrication.

ABOVE
George Daniels at his desk.

After three years of trial and error he submitted a movement to the Chronometer Department of the Royal Observatory at Hurstmonceux for testing. It was found to register zero variation under the most stringent tests. After another two years' work, Daniels was sufficiently satisfied with the design to patent it – under the name "Co-axial Escapement."

George Daniels is the author of several publications. The *Art of Breguet; Watchmaking* (1981) sets out to describe and illustrate every aspect of the subject in uncomplicated terms; he also privately produced a limited edition of *The Practical Watch Escapement*, which illustrates his unique co-axial escapement along with others. While accepting the accuracy of electronic watches ("until the battery commits suicide"), Daniels is convinced that there is a discerning public which is not interested in splitting seconds, but prefers the elegance and beauty of a fine mechanical watch, the result of hundreds of years of development and the loving care of a master craftsman.

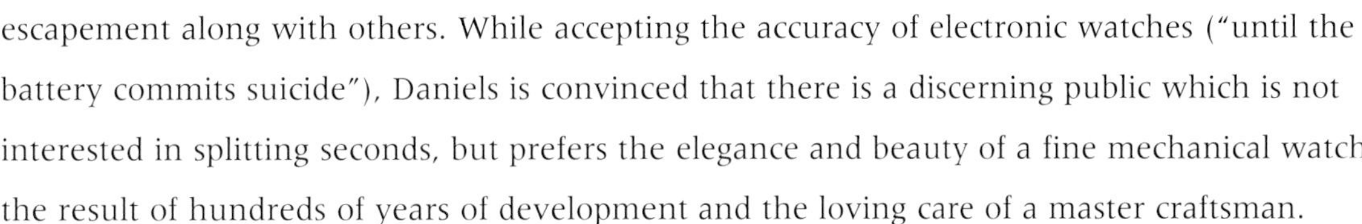

The majority of Daniels' creations are pocket watches, simply because that is the size of watch he prefers to make. But when it was suggested that his co-axial escapement could not be fitted into a wristwatch, he promptly set out to design and make one.

The model illustrated is a double-sided wristwatch which shows the normal hours, minutes, and seconds; by pressing a button on the side of the case band, the inner case reverses to reveal a month and date calendar and a one-minute tourbillon with Daniels' co-axial escapement.

Another wristwatch features a four-minute tourbillon with subsidiary chronograph and co-axial escapement. The second photograph shows the tourbillon. Both watches have 18-karat gold cases, silver and gold dials, and gold hands; every single part was made by Daniels in his own workshop without assistance.

There is no George Daniels Flagship and no product line since each watch is made individually. Daniels says he doesn't make watches to sell, but to please himself. When he has finished one – usually after about a year's work – a buyer is always waiting, however high the price.

№16

DUNHILL

Alfred Dunhill was basically a shopkeeper, albeit one who catered for a largely aristocratic clientele who patronized the shop which he opened in London's St. James's area in 1907. The company itself, however, was already 14 years old and as early as 1903 had made an application to patent a dashboard clock.

ABOVE

CENTENARY

Parchment Dial Centenary Arabic numerals combined with index and blue hands provide a distinctive face.

Although best known originally for smokers' requisites – tobacco, the famous Dunhill White Spot pipes, the distinctive lighters – Dunhill soon established a reputation for purveying luxury products which its founder described as "useful, beautiful, dependable and the best of their kind." A 1906 pocket watch perfectly illustrates this style – a double-sided timepiece incorporating a tachymeter. Subsequently the firm produced a watch lighter (1926), a watch belt (1929), and a watch pencil (1936).

As the firm approached its century, its selection of watches increased in both scope and design. Now part of the Vendôme luxury goods group which includes Cartier, Baume et Mercier, and Piaget, Dunhill has access to some of the most modern watch production facilities in Switzerland.

To celebrate its centenary, Dunhill introduced a line of mechanical watches in 18-karat gold rectangular cases with an Art Deco look on classic black lizard straps. Hand-finished steel versions followed a year later. 1994 also saw the launch of the Londinium collection, fitted with quartz movements in round cases with hour markings on the bezel.

There was a GMT version which enabled a second and third time zone to be read by independent hands which was also a certified chronometer. A sports model in the line has unidirectional bezel and tritium hands and dial.

A later collection, the Millenium, has a very recognizable round profile

ABOVE

LONDINIUM

The line now includes this all polished steel version, equipped with a Swiss quartz movement.

RIGHT

AD 2000

Distinctive navy blue dial watch, with precision timing guaranteed by the fine quartz movement.

PRODUCT RANGE

Centenary
Millenium
Londinium
AD 2000

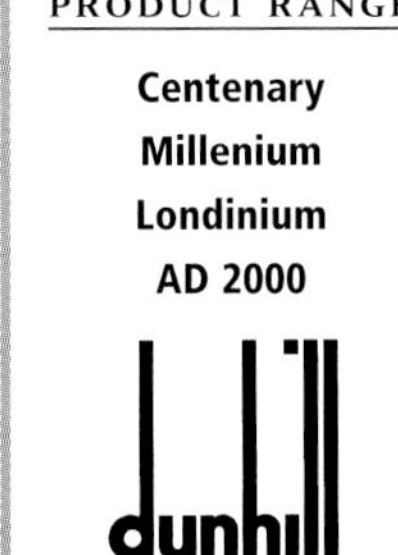

ABOVE
Dunhill creates innovative products that in time become classics. This hexagonal watch is based on a 1920s design, the earliest Dunhill watch.

with very small neat strap and bracelet attachments. There is a sports model in two-toned brushed and polished steel, and a chronograph with moonphase as well as the customary elapsed time recorders and 1/10 second-timing facility.

The latest from Dunhill is the AD 2000 collection, a line of six models with a unique curved steel case with distinctive markings like a snake's head. They are offered on an all-steel bracelet or leather strap, and have a high-quality Swiss quartz movement. They have sapphire crystals and are water resistant to 165 feet. The collection was inspired by the work of British designers in such diverse fields as architecture, automobiles, household items, and transportation.

Dunhill, Britain's sole luxury product manufacturer, markets its products through 40 Dunhill stores throughout the world and a vast network of approved retailers.

ABOVE
18kt gold Dunhill watch with raised gold numerals on dial. c. 1936.

FLAGSHIP LINE

The Millenium collection is Dunhill's best-known line. It has many variations, which nevertheless retain a family look because of its unusual bracelet or strap fastening. Its best example is the Chronograph. Its classic dial with Roman figures and three sub-dials is viewed through a sapphire crystal; it records 10 1/10 secs and has a tachymeter around the main dial. Its mechanical self-winding movement has a power reserve of 50 hours, and its case is brushed steel and gold plate. There is a choice of white or black dial with gilt hands and figures.

LEFT
MILLENIUM
The popular Millenium Sports in an all steel finish.

FACT FILE

FOUNDED: 1893
COUNTRY OF ORIGIN: England
OUTPUT: Approximately 40,000 per annum
MOVEMENT: Mechanical and quartz slimline
CHAIRMAN: Richard Dunhill
CEO: Mr. François Poriel

EBEL

The "Fabrique Ebel, Blum et Cie" was founded in 1911 by Eugène Blum, who made up the name from his initials and those of his wife Alice's family name – Eugéne Blum Et Levy – EBEL. The brand first came to prominence when it won a gold medal at the Swiss National Exhibition in 1914.

Eugène concentrated on the quality of production of his watches and then traveled the world to sell them; Alice looked after the business and contributed to the designs. Their son Charles took over in 1929 and was followed – somewhat reluctantly it seems – by his son Pierre-Alain in 1970.

Pierre-Alain was a marketing man and introduced new lines into what had become a fairly conventional, if technically sound, collection. His Sports collection was a great success; then followed the Beluga line, which had several versions, including an automatic with day and date. In the late 1970s, the firm acquired and restored a Turkish villa in La Chaux de Fonds which had been designed by the famous architect Le Corbusier, who had been born in the town. Inspired by these surroundings, Pierre-Alain created the concept of the "Architects of Time," which has been the theme of the company's collections ever since.

PRODUCT RANGE

Sports
– Classic
– Discovery
– Voyager
1911
Beluga
Lichine
Modulor
Shanta

EBEL

BELOW
SPORTWAVE
Sportwave Ladies quartz watch in bicolor with steel bracelet.

RIGHT
1911
A large gasket provides water-resistance for the back of this 18kt gold 1911's three-part watch case.

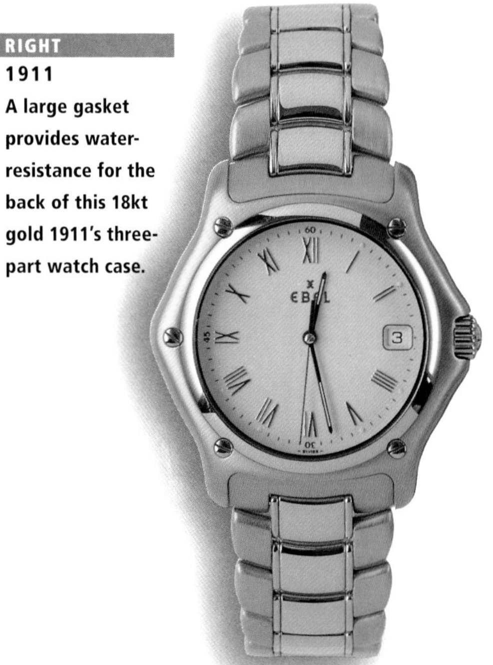

RIGHT
CHRONOGRAPH
18kt gold case, mother-of-pearl and diamonds dial. Automatic chronograph movement. Scratch resistant sapphire glass.

LEFT
The Beluga line: the round Beluga and two new shapes, Tonneau and Carrée, made only of gold and available in a single size.

ABOVE
This Beluga watch is available in three sizes and has interchangeable dial and bezel, 18kt gold bracelet or choice of strap.

The line includes both quartz and mechanical movements, made in Ebel's own Swiss factory or built exclusively to their specification. Typical lines are the Beluga, with distinctive double-curve 18-karat gold cases with quartz movements, mother-of-pearl dials, and chunky bracelets. A variation is the Beluga-Lichine, with a self-winding movement and double barrel mainsprings.

LEFT
Shanta, inspired by Indian mythology. Shanta the serene was the flower of creation, ruling the emotions with grace and sensitivity.

Le Modulor, which took five years to develop, is an automatic chronograph with chronometer rating. In 18-karat gold, gold and steel, or all steel, it has a high frequency 28,800 vph balance and is water-resistant to 165 feet.

To mark its 75th anniversary, Ebel created the 1911, a rounded version of its original Sport, in 18-karat gold or gold and steel, with a choice of quartz or mechanical movement. The latest model is the Shanta, named after a goddess of Indian mythology who was the ideal of womanhood. Its 18-karat gold case has a hinged cover over the mother-of-pearl dial and is integral with the decorative bracelet; it has a quartz movement and is water-resistant to 100 feet.

ABOVE

Lichine – available in steel or 18kt gold with a choice of twin-barrel automatic movement or automatic with power reserve indicator.

ABOVE

Le Modulor. An automatic chronograph with chronometer rating, which took five years to develop.

FLAGSHIP LINE

The Sports collection was Ebel's first successful line, and its successor the Sportwave is still one of its most popular collections. The Classic, with the characteristic Ebel wave bracelet, is the star; there is also a Classic Discovery diver's watch, the Voyager – an automatic watch with two time-zones, and a Perpetual Calendar Chronograph. The Sportswave models are designed to bring Ebel's quality and finish within reach of a younger and more active public.

LEFT

EBEL SPORTS CLASSIC

Steel case and bracelet, water-resistant to 100ft.

FACT FILE

FOUNDED: 1911
COUNTRY OF ORIGIN: Switzerland
OUTPUT: Information not available
MOVEMENT: Mechanical and quartz
CEO: Pierre-Alain Blum

№18

Eterna

Eterna has its origins in 1851 in Grenchen in the foothills of the Jura Mountains, where Josef Girard, the local doctor, and a farmer, Anton Schild, concerned to find work for the many unemployed young people of the village, proposed a plan to have them apprenticed to watchmakers in the region. Later the two employed them, with municipal backing, to make watch parts. The plan folded, but Girard would not be deterred. In 1856 Girard and Anton's son Urs, a schoolteacher, set up a factory to make watch parts. In due course they started making movement blanks and then complete watches.

Their persistence paid off. In 1906 Theodore Schild, Urs' grandson, registered the company as "Fabriques Eterna," and the name, which had been on the dials for some time, was officially established. In 1914 Eterna produced the first wristwatch with an alarm, in 1926 the first watch-cigarette lighter, and in 1930 the smallest mass-produced wristwatch with a baguette movement.

In 1932 Theodore split the company into two divisions – ETA SA for the production of movement blanks, and Eterna SA for the manufacture of precision watches.

Ten years later, Eterna went into quantity production with a self-winding movement of very compact dimensions – 22mm across and only 4.5mm thick. But what really established Eterna internationally was the development of a ball-bearing mounted rotor for self-winding movements. Called the Eterna·Matic, it set new standards for automatic wristwatches. The company made the five balls of the system Eterna's trademark.

For its 100th anniversary in 1956, Eterna launched the Centenaire, which became one of its greatest series successes, and followed this with an Eterna·Matic Kontiki, one of the original sports watches, with water-resistance of 660 feet. The company had supplied Thor Heyerdahl's crew with Eterna wristwatches when they crossed the Pacific in a balsa boat in 1947. By 1962 the Eterna·matic 3000 had become the world's slimmest automatic at 3.4mm.

Eterna was one of the first companies to see the possibilities of quartz; the Eterna Sonic was

ABOVE
KONTIKI
Steel case and bracelet, with quartz movement and luminous dial and hands.

ABOVE
ETERNA·MATIC
Features self-winding movement, luminous dials and hands and scratch-resistant sapphire crystal.

LEFT
LES HISTORIQUES
Striking rectangular watch based on 1935 design. Case in 18kt rose gold.

PRODUCT RANGE

Kontiki
1956
Les Historiques
Eterna·Matic
Athena
Galaxis

launched in 1970, followed by the Royal Quartz Kontiki in 1976. The next four years saw a succession of "firsts," culminating in the award of the *Grand Prix Triomphe de l'Excellence Européene* sponsored by the Nobel Peace prize-winner René Cassin. Eterna had achieved international recognition.

In 1984 the PCW group took over Eterna – previously part of the SMH conglomerate – and appointed Herbert Arni, a former head of the Omega Division of SMH to manage the company. The final move came in 1995 when Eterna was acquired by a company owned by the industrialist E. A. Porsche, a stipulation being that the management remained in place.

To celebrate its 140th anniversary, Eterna has produced a limited edition of the famous 1935 model in rose gold and stainless steel. Among its current collections, Les Historiques includes replicas of the 1935 original, the 1948 Eterna·Matic, the Alarm with automatic movement – also 1948 vintage – and Airforce I, based on one made for aviators in 1936. All these beautiful watches are collector's items.

The Pininfarina line of sports watches resulted from collaboration with the famous designer's studio and includes a diver's watch and a chronograph. There is a new line of Kontiki watches, including a lady's automatic model and a Super Diver's model. And there is the Galaxis collection, in 18-karat gold cases and bracelets set with specially treated sapphires in deep rich blue. The dials are plain blue or have diamond hour markers. All have quartz movements.

LEFT

ETERNA SUPER KONTIKI

FLAGSHIP LINE

Kontiki, started in 1947, when Thor Heyerdahl approached Eterna for watches for his spectacular adventure. From the small number of specially prepared models has grown a hugely successful collection. Eterna·Matic Kontiki models are available in steel or gold, with quartz or mechanical movements, chronometer certificates, scratch resistance, sapphire crystals, and are water-resistant up to 1,000 feet (Super Kontiki) or 400 feet (chronograph).

FACT FILE

FOUNDED: 1856
COUNTRY OF ORIGIN: Switzerland
OUTPUT: Information not available
MOVEMENT: Mechanical 50%, quartz 50%
CEO: Herbert W. Arni

№19

FORTIS

Fortis was launched in 1912 in Grenchen by Walter Vogt, who began by making gold-cased mechanical watches.

In 1926 Vogt met John Harwood, the Englishman who in 1924 invented the first self-winding wristwatch. Finding no interested manufacturer in England, he had patented his device in Switzerland. There was no crown on the original prototype; the hands were set by means of a rotating, fluted bezel. A red point, seen through an opening in the dial, indicated that the watch was functioning. Vogt immediately saw the possibility of Harwood's invention, and at the Basel Trade Fair in 1926 Fortis launched the world's first automatic watch in serial production (there had been a small limited series previously).

Fortis went on to build up a reputation for making sturdy automatic watches – in fact, one early advertisement shows a watch with the name Fortissimo. Lady Hay, a British journalist, took one on the *Graf Zeppelin's* first voyage around the world.

Another Fortis benchmark was the introduction in 1968 of the Flipper, a colorful line of fun watches, with water-resistant plastic cases, interchangeable straps, and even bezels and quartz analog movements. Pre-Swatch, it was one of the pioneers of the "pop watch" era.

The Fortis official Cosmonaut's Chronograph was developed in intensive cooperation with the Yuri Gagarin Cosmonauts Training Center in the Russian Star City and has been part of the official equipment of the European–Russian space mission since 1994. During the Soyuz 19 mission it even ventured outside the space station with no ill effects at all, and subsequently it received a Russian diploma certifying its fitness for space.

ABOVE
CHRONOGRAPH
Official Cosmonaut's Chronograph – Diver – designed specifically for use during diving.

ABOVE
HARWOOD
In 18kt gold, named after the inventor of the world's first automatic wristwatch.

LEFT
PILOT'S CHRONOGRAPH
A distinctive functional design with a clear, easy-to-read black dial.

PRODUCT RANGE

Cosmonaut's chronograph
Pilot
Diver
GMT Chronometer
Pilot's Chronograph
Flipper
Harwood

There is also a Fortis Pilot chronograph in steel, which has a similar specification but with a bidirectional turning bezel. A Diver chronograph has the same movement with a unidirectional bezel. Both are water-resistant to 330 feet.

Also in the line is a GMT chronometer with COSC certificate and an additional 24-hour small hand which is adjustable to give a second time zone, and a Pilot's GMT chronometer fitted with an ETA 7750 movement with a special construction. To mark the 70th anniversary of Vogt's historic meeting, the Harwood Watch Company – a separate company in the Fortis empire – has brought out a replica of John Harwood's watch, now fitted with a hand-finished Swiss movement – the ETA 2092 – specially adapted so that it can be wound just like the original by the knurled bezel. There is a choice of 18-karat gold, steel, steel and gold, or sterling silver for the case; there is even a platinum version, in which the characteristic red dot is replaced by a blue one. All these models are individually numbered.

ABOVE
Official Cosmonaut's Chronograph – GMT Chronometer. This comes with COSC certificate and an additional 24-hr small hand, adjustable to give a second time zone.

ABOVE
Official Cosmonaut's Chronograph – Cosmonaut – in 18kt gold with leather strap.

FACT FILE

FOUNDED: **1912**
COUNTRY OF ORIGIN: **Switzerland**
OUTPUT: **Information not available**
MOVEMENT: **Mechanical and quartz**
CEO: **Peter Peter**

FLAGSHIP LINE

In 1996, for the 35th anniversary of the first manned space flight in 1961, Fortis have produced an 18-karat gold version of the Cosmonaut's Chronograph with an automatic 28,800 vph movement, day, date, and 24-hour indicators, and a 60-minute counter. Its steel case has a screwdown crown, pusher, and back; it is water-resistant to 330 feet and has glareproof sapphire crystals on the front and back. The tachymeter scale is on the bezel. Each watch is individually numbered, and a limited edition of 100 models has been produced. (Model 602.50.11 illustrated)

LEFT
LIMITED EDITION COSMONAUT'S CHRONOGRAPH

№20

Gerald Genta

Although Gerald Genta gives the impression of being a one-man band, the company in fact has two centers of production – one in Geneva, the other in Le Brassus – and employs 120 people. The master himself admittedly conceives and designs each new watch from his apartment in Monte Carlo.

ABOVE
BLUE CRYSTAL
The Jewel-watch with internally faceted glass.

Gerald Genta was originally a designer of watches for some of the Great Houses and at the same time made a certain number of commissioned special pieces for rich clients. In 1969 he conceived the idea of producing his designs commercially, beginning audaciously at the top with a selection of simple designs in precious metal cases, with his personal design touch on each of them.

Once Gerald Genta has designed a watch, the drawings are passed to the team of technicians in le Brassus or Geneva who, with the aid of micromechanical processes and computer technology, turn them into the necessary gears, pinions, and other parts, often meticulously finished by hand, that go to make up a Gerald Genta watch. Sometimes the intricacy of the movement means that it takes months, or even years, before the piece is ready to leave the factory, and such is the degree of hand work involved that no two pieces are identical.

Gerald Genta's young team of specialists in Geneva is headed by chief watchmaker Paul Michel Golay, one of the city's special commissioners who can grant the right to inscribe a watch movement with the coveted "Poinçon de Genève."

His most prestigious wristwatch is the Quantième Perpetual with a minute repeater, tourbillon, and universal time. There have been many variants, and early examples are eagerly sought by collectors at auctions.

Another remarkable creation was the Blue Crystal, which has an internally faceted glass

ABOVE
FANTASIES
Minnie Mouse points out the time in this novelty watch.

LEFT
GEFICA SAFARI
The watch designed at the request of three hunting enthusiasts.

PRODUCT RANGE

Fantasies
Success
Gefica Safari
L'Octo
Blue Crystal
Quantième Perpetual
Retro Fantasy
Grande Sonnerie

gērald genta

through which the delicate blue shade of the dial, made from rare Namibian onyx, makes its unique appearance. The model is available in simple automatic form or with a perpetual calendar and moonphase. Current models range from Success, in octagonal cases of 18-karat gold, gold and steel, or all steel on a strap or bracelet, with automatic chronograph or quartz movements and a unique black carbon-fiber dial, to the Fantasies collection with Mickey Mouse or Donald Duck on mother-of-pearl dials in 18-karat gold cases – surely the first time these characters have appeared in such upscale surroundings!

ABOVE
Grande Sonnerie has a complete chiming mechanism – striking either with minute repetition or for hours and quarter hours.

ABOVE
A mechanism of the Quantieme Perpetual with Tourbilllon Minute Repeater. The winder is sculpted and stylized by the two opposite "G's".

The Gefica Safari, created at the request of three hunting friends, has a unique case of gunbarrel bronze and an automatic chronograph movement. For those not quite so addicted to the woods, there is a gold-cased version with quartz movement and an alarm function.

Realizing that there are many people with the discernment to appreciate his unique creations, but that not all are able to afford such horological masterpieces, Gerald Genta has designed L'Octo, which blends a round case with the softened lines of an octagon. It carries the firm's pearled crown trademark and comes with quartz or mechanical hand-wound or automatic movement in an 18-karat gold or steel case on a strap, and is designed to offer a more affordable model to a wider customer base.

FACT FILE

FOUNDED: 1969
COUNTRY OF ORIGIN: Switzerland
OUTPUT: Information not available
MOVEMENT: Quartz and mechanical
CEO: Gerald Genta

FLAGSHIP LINE

Gerald Genta reckons the Success design is typical of his touch – a totally new concept in case design, in the treatment of the dial and crystal, and in its ability to adapt to quartz, mechanical, hand-wound, automatic, or even chronograph, movements.

RIGHT
SUCCESS

Nº21

GIRARD PERREGAUX

Girard Perregaux can trace its beginnings back to Geneva in 1791 when Jean François Bautte, who had started work at the age of 12, at 19 created two beautiful watches which caused his employer Jacques Dauphin to make him a partner. By 1830 his firm was employing 300 workers, and its products – movements, cases, dials, and jeweled watches – were well known and highly regarded.

ABOVE

LIGNE CLASSIQUE

From the classic line, classic simplicity and elegance.

ABOVE

LIGNE 7000

Automatic, mechanical chronograph, from a wide selection in this line.

Bautte specialized in ultraflat watches which gained him many rich and important clients. After his death in 1837, the firm passed to his son and then went through a variety of changes of name as it passed down to various members of the family until, in 1906, it was inherited by Constant Girard Gallet.

Girard Gallet had founded a watch company in La Chaux de Fonds in 1852 with his brother Numa. Two years later, he married Marie Perregaux – also from a watchmaking family – and renamed the firm Girard Perregaux. Their watches were very beautiful and won many prizes; they were also favorites of the clergy, who had them set in crosses of precious stones.

In 1897 the firm received an order from the German Navy for 2,000 of the new "wristwatches" – the world's first mass-produced ones – which were a great success, though when they tried to export them to the United States, they were not well received. Constant died in 1903; his son Constant Junior succeeded him and over the next fifty years built up the firm's reputation for high-precision chronometers. In 1967, 73 percent of the chronometers tested by the Neuchâtel Observatory were of Girard Perregaux's manufacture.

After World War II, the firm, known for its technical research, patented the Gyromatic (1957), a device which allows for very flat automatics, and produced movements with increasingly high frequency – up to 36,000 vph. Girard Perregaux was one of the first of the great houses to venture into electronics, producing its own quartz

LEFT

LIGNE RICHEVILLE

Handwound mechanical Chronograph. Available in yellow or white gold, or steel case with white gold bezel.

PRODUCT RANGE

Laureato Olimpico
Vintage 1996
Tonneau
Ferrari
Tourbillon Chronograph
Richeville
Ligne Classique
Ligne 7000

Girard-Perregaux

movements in 1969, and in 1970 launching its first quartz watch. By 1978 an extra-flat quartz model was in production, and by 1983 85 percent of all quartz watches granted a certificate of precision from Neuchâtel were made by Girard Perregaux, making a unique double.

ABOVE
Vintage 1996 Chronograph. The limited edition Vintage collection forms a tribute to each classic creation of the early 20th century.

Production at this time was a blend of electronics and traditional watchmaking. The firm produced quartz models of great complexity, like the Equation, whose multiple functions were controlled by a single crown, but Girard Perregaux's heart was in the creation of complicated mechanical masterpieces.

Back in 1850, Constant Girard had designed a pocket watch chronometer with three straight bridges and a tourbillon escapement. It brought him immediate fame and, in 1855, a Gold Medal at the Paris World Fair. In 1867, after gold had been adjudged the most suitable material from which to make the bridges, the company (now known as Girard Perregaux) brought out a Tourbillon with Three Golden Bridges, which won an award at the Paris Exposition the same year and again in 1889. In 1901 it was judged to be too perfect to compete.

ABOVE
The Tourbillon with three gold bridges won Constant Girard-Perregaux two gold medals at the Paris Universal Exhibition in 1867, and later in 1889.

In 1982 the firm's watchmakers decided to produce 20 examples of the watch, identical in every respect to the original. Since it took eight months to produce one watch, it is not surprising that the last of the series was not completed until 1990. The following year, the master watchmakers undertook the task of building a wristwatch version. They succeeded, but understandably the Tourbillon with Three Golden Bridges wristwatch was produced in very limited series and is now a prized collector's item.

Since then, Girard Perregaux has created, every year, a new wristwatch design based on the Three Bridges. For the firm's 205th anniversary, it has combined the technicality of the three bridges construction with the complexity of its own mechanical chronograph movement – a unique construction, the fascinating mechanics of which can be seen through the unusual transparent crystal case back.

Another retrospective model is the Vintage Chronograph 1996. Based on a 1960s design, it is available in yellow, pink, or white gold, and its golden rotor is visible through a sapphire crystal back.

Since the turn of the century, Girard Perregaux has brought out a watch to mark each Olympic year. In 1996 the model took the form of the Laureato Olimpico in a stainless-steel case on an integrated bracelet in a series limited to 999 pieces. There is a "Laureato for Ladies" in a similar case embellished with diamonds and baguette-cut precious stones.

ABOVE

The "Tribute to Ferrari" Chronograph is available in stainless-steel, steel, steel and gold and 18kt gold.

The Richeville Tonneau chronograph with a manual-wind movement was launched in 1995 and for 1996 has an automatic movement; the cases come in the usual variety of materials, and there is a choice of dials.

FLAGSHIP LINE

When the Italian car manufacturer Ferrari decided in 1993 to launch a watch collection, it was natural that its president should look to his racing driver friend Luigi Macaluso, who was president of Girard Perregaux. The collection started with a split-second chronograph mainly in 18-karat white gold on a strap. Later came a stainless-steel automatic chronograph with a flyback hand and date; currently, this bestselling sports line is also available in steel, steel and gold, and 18-karat gold with snugly fitting bracelets.

RIGHT

FERRARI
Chronograph with fly-back hand. Limited edition tribute to Ferrari.

FACT FILE

FOUNDED: 1791
COUNTRY OF ORIGIN: Switzerland
OUTPUT: 15,000 pieces per annum
MOVEMENT: Mechanical 90%, quartz 10%
CEO: Luigi Macaluso

Gucci

Gucci watches are marketed by the Severin Group, which was founded by Severin Wunderman in 1972. With a production of over a million watches a year, it claims to be Switzerland's third largest manufacturer of watches. The group holds the worldwide licence to manufacture and distribute Gucci watches.

Severin Wunderman had the idea of applying a fashion house to a watch collection; he chose Gucci because its products had the style and elegance he wished to recreate in his watches. His personal credo is "We don't submit to fashion, we create it," and he has been the inspiration of a fashion-focused line of timepieces which has had a quite phenomenal success.

Gucci itself began in 1922 when Guccio Gucci opened a boutique in Florence to sell his leather goods and equestrian accessories, which he identified by the initials "GG." His enterprise became an international success story, and his boutiques – by now worldwide – were patronized by the great and the good – famous actresses, political women, even royalty. Its image of quality made it an ideal vehicle on which to launch a line of top-quality, well-designed Swiss watches. In 1989 the Severin Group transferred its production headquarters to Lengnau in

PRODUCT RANGE

3600
5500
6600
7400
9040
9750
1700

GUCCI

BELOW
9040
Quartz movement with bicolor stainless steel and gold-plated case and champagne dial.

RIGHT
6300 L
Gold plated with leather strap and mother-of-pearl dial. Quartz movement.

RIGHT
3000 L
Gold plated with leather strap and distinctive red and green striped dial. Quartz movement.

RIGHT
The 6600 line. The ancient coin on the back of these watches recalls the ancient legend of Alpheus and Arethusa.

ABOVE
Model 7400 Automatic. This limited edition has a stainless steel case with crystal case back showing the movement. The dial is silver or pink copper.

Switzerland. In 1993 the Gucci family interests were sold to an international investment group, but the connection with the Severin Group remained intact.

The success of the group has been based on sound marketing principles, which were put into practice first in the United States, still its number one market, with 51 percent of global sales. Extensive testing in the marketplace has always been a priority, and Severin Wunderman is very much involved in the initial design of new models.

Among Gucci's current models are the "5500," the designation of a pair of watch cases shaped like intertwining horseshoes – a legacy from Gucci's equestrian heritage. Silver dials with delicate Roman figures give a classical look to this model, which comes in stainless steel or PVD gold. It has a date window at 3 o'clock, is water-resistant to 100 feet, and has a Swiss quartz movement. It comes on a strap or steel link bracelet.

LEFT
Model 5500 in gents and ladies versions, with stainless steel case, black and silver dial, stainless steel bracelet or simulated crocodile strap.

The 6600 – also known as the Syracusa – has a reversible case featuring a replica of an ancient Greek coin in pewter on the back; the Gucci name takes the place of numerals. It has a quartz movement, a sapphire crystal, and the water-resistant case is gold plated to 10 micron.

ABOVE
Model 9040 in gents and ladies versions, with ETA quartz movement. The dials come in slate, ivory or champagne.

The 7400 – all Gucci models are identified by numbers rather than names – is a limited edition man's automatic timepiece with ETA 2892 movement with date and center seconds. It has a polished stainless steel case and is available on a strap or bracelet.

The 9040 comes in two sizes – man's and lady's – in steel and 10 micron gold-plated bicolor cases with matching chunky bracelets. There is a choice of three dial finishes, the movement is a Swiss ETA quartz, and both models have a date window at 6 o'clock. Finally the 9750 is a 330-foot diver's watch in a substantial stainless-steel case with screwback, sapphire crystal, and unidirectional rotating bezel. Tritium hands and hour markers are bold enough to see at depth, and there is a choice of stainless-steel bracelet with security clasp or sharkskin strap. It has a quartz movement.

FACT FILE

FOUNDED: 1972
COUNTRY OF ORIGIN: Switzerland
OUTPUT: 1,000,000 units per annum
MOVEMENT: Quartz 90%, automatic 10%
CEO: Severin Wunderman

Another major concept in fashion watches is the model 1700 for ladies, in which the steel or 18-karat gold-plated case can be removed from the colored carbonite bracelet by a 45-degree twist. The watch head can be replaced by a "G," disk so the bracelet can be worn on its own. The watch comes with three bracelets, and additional ones can be purchased separately. It has an ETA quartz movement.

As with any main fashion product, Gucci watches are subject to counterfeiting, which it combats vigorously throughout the world; its surveillance is helped by its computerized serial number documentation.

BELOW
3600

FLAGSHIP LINE

Outstanding is the recently launched 3600; its square case, shaped like the letter "G," is the work of designer Tom Ford. Its polished stainless-steel case comes in three sizes, and there is a stainless-steel chunky link bracelet with a unique double push-button clasp. A sapphire crystal and screwback guarantee its water-resistance to 100 feet.

№23

HUBLOT

Carlo Crocco, President of MDM Genève, is a man with a concept. He comes from a watchmaking family – his grandfather was a watchmaker who founded a successful firm in Italy nearly a hundred years ago. Carlo himself set up the firm of Breil, which combined Italian flair for style with Swiss technology and established him in the watch industry.

ABOVE
AUTOMATIC
Hublot automatic with traditional Hublot rubber strap.

But he saved his best idea for the firm he founded in Geneva in 1980 – Hublot. The name, in French, means "porthole," and the simple round case with the tiny titanium screws on the bezel at the numerical points is very reminiscent of a ship's window on the world. But his unique idea was to combine this classical design, in its water-protected case of precious metal, with a rubber strap of such composition that it would be equally at home on a Mediterranean beach or a table at the Four Seasons.

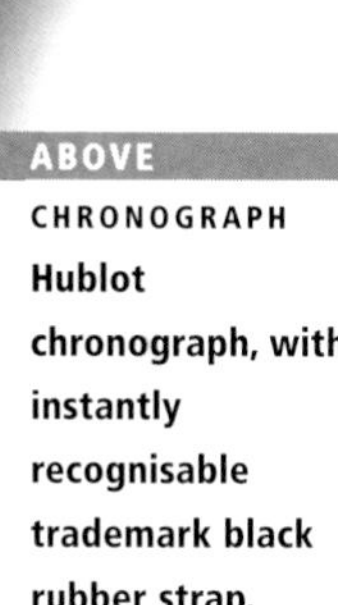

ABOVE
CHRONOGRAPH
Hublot chronograph, with instantly recognisable trademark black rubber strap.

The bracelet, naturally, is no ordinary rubber band. It took three years to research and develop its supple resilience and sensuous satin finish with steel fastening inserts at the bezel and clasp. These unusual straps are made in Italy exclusively for Hublot, and they are therefore the only part of the watch not entirely Swiss.

Crocco's other attribute is his consistency. For the first ten years, he kept the same basic case design, offering only a choice of size and material – steel, steel and gold, or 18-karat gold. Hublot watches have what MDM claims is a unique water-resistant system, especially on the crown, and the collection includes both quartz models with top ETA movements and the very best automatic mechanical movements, introduced in 1988 from specialists such as Frédéric Piquet at Le Brassus.

PRODUCT RANGE

Hublot
Automatic
Chronograph
Diver
Frog-Motif
Greenwich Mean Time

MDM
GENEVE

RIGHT
GREENWICH MEAN TIME
Quartz movement, bi-directional with a bezel marked in 24hrs.

Carlo Crocco admits his watches are not for the ordinary man – they reflect a lifestyle, he says, that revolves around dynamism and efficiency while not neglecting the pleasures of beauty. But he insists they are not for collectors; they are practical watches, which are meant to be used and worn.

BELOW
Every Hublot watch can now be fitted with the new "Colonial" mesh bracelet as an attractive alternative to the original black rubber strap.

The Hublot collection includes chronographs and diver's models with automatic movements and steel or gold cases, water-resistant to 1,000 feet, and there is a Greenwich Mean Time design for world travelers which gives a second time zone.

FACT FILE

FOUNDED: 1980
COUNTRY OF ORIGIN: Switzerland
OUTPUT: Information not available
MOVEMENT: Mechanical and quartz
CEO: Carlo Crocco

Hublot has also been experimenting with dials enhanced by champlevé enamel, a traditional technique that was once the prerogative of Geneva's craftsmen; it is still mastered by only a handful of experts. The technique has been applied to a number of different designs: one is a "frog" theme, on a green or a blue ground in very limited numbers – just 30 each. The watches have automatic movements, 18-karat yellow or white-gold cases, water-resistant to 165 feet and, of course, the traditional Hublot strap.

And just to show that the famous rubber strap is not indispensable, Hublot has produced a "Colonial" mesh bracelet of unusually refined construction, its 240 components held together by screws to give an extremely comfortable fit. The international jury of journalists at the 1996 Basel Fair were so impressed by its comfort and originality that without hesitation they awarded it the prize for "The Best" bracelet. It is available in steel, steel and gold, and solid 18-karat gold.

RIGHT
GREEN/BLUE DIALS

FLAGSHIP LINE

The company's latest creations have dials in muted colors – a rich emerald green or a vibrant royal blue – toned down by fine honeycomb texturing which gives a more refined touch. They have quartz movements, a sapphire crystal, and are water-resistant to 165 feet.

Ingersoll

Robert Ingersoll staked his claim to a place in horological history when, in 1892, he launched his Dollar watch, one a working man could buy for a day's pay. He called it the Yankee, gave away a chain with it, and advertised it as the "Watch that made the dollar famous."

ABOVE

NURSE FOB

In addition to the classic white dial, Nurse Fob also comes in blue, or with a luminous dial for night duty.

His earlier model, which he called the Universal, sold for a dollar and a half; it took him two years to reach his goal.

Ingersoll was soon in large-scale production. In 1901 a London wholesaler gave the firm an order for a million watches; part of it was for a South African Boer War souvenir watch with a picture of Queen Victoria on the dial, surrounded by her Generals. Four years later, Ingersoll set up an office in London, sold his Dollar watch for five shillings and called it the Crown. It was wound by the stem – earlier ones had a butterfly key in the back – and he guaranteed his watches for a year.

Another early success was his wristwatch for the soldiers in World War I. Adapted from a lady's pocket watch, it was sold with a protective grid over the dial. Other models had luminous hands and numbers, a new idea. He christened his invention Radiolite, and by 1918 more than 85 percent of Ingersoll watches had Radiolite dials.

The London House of Ingersoll, as it was called, had been importing most of its watches from the United States, but during the war the firm started assembling them in London. By 1922 it was producing 3,000 pieces a day. Ingersoll became a household word, and many famous people – Mark Twain the writer, Sir Alan Cobham the aviator,

PRODUCT RANGE

Radio Controlled
Chronographs
Diver's
Men's Dress
Gents Bracelet
Ladies' Bracelet
Nurse Fob
Children's models
Ladies Strap
Gents Strap

ABOVE

LADIES BRACELET

One from a varied range of elegant ladies watches.

LEFT

LADIES STRAP WATCHES

Ladies strap watches have a more practical look.

Thomas Edison the inventor, and many more, were not ashamed to wear an inexpensive Ingersoll – quite the opposite.

In the Great Depression of the 1930s, the London directors bought out the American owners, and Ingersoll became a wholly owned British public company.

In 1933 the company pioneered the world's first character watch, a Mickey Mouse watch, which was an instant bestseller.

On the outbreak of World War II, the company produced watches for the services and then turned to aircraft parts and locks. In the closing stages of the war, the British Government brought together three firms – Ingersoll, Smiths, and Vickers – and set aside £1 million to establish a watch factory in South Wales; the first watches came off the line in 1947.

The early models were based on Ingersoll's famous "five-bob" pocket watches, but later men's, women's, boys' and girls' watches were added. Ingersoll introduced a number of specialist watches; it pioneered the Pop Watch scene with a line of "Trendsetters" and produced a Coronation model which, along with many of the company's earlier designs, are now collectors' items. In 1960 the firm sold its interest in the Welsh factory and began to import Swiss watches once again – up to 600,000 a year. One of the very first quartz analog watches produced in Switzerland had Ingersoll on the dial.

Toward the end of the 1960s, the Heron Corporation acquired a majority shareholding in the firm. They then proceeded to sell it to the Zeon Group, one of Britain's largest watch distributors, a few years later.

LEFT
In addition to the classic round face, ladies bracelet watches also come with this streamlined rectangular case.

Ingersoll's current collection consists of some 100 models, ranging from chunky men's chronographs, diver's models, and slim dress watches to ladies' watches with a variety of bracelets. And to keep up with the latest developments, there is a solar-powered model for men. All Ingersoll watches are quartz and carry a three-year guarantee.

FLAGSHIP LINE

Ingersoll's flagship must surely be the Nurse Fob. Introduced in the early 1950s, it has been hugely popular with several generations of nurses. It has gone through a number of minor changes, but remains basically the same. The present models include one with inbuilt luminescence, a boon to nurses on night duty.

FACT FILE

FOUNDED: 1892
COUNTRY OF ORIGIN: United States, England
OUTPUT: 300,000 per annum
MOVEMENT: All quartz
CEO: Richard Tibber

RIGHT
NURSE FOB

IWC The International Watch Co.

In the 1860s another American who was to make a lasting impression on the Swiss watch scene visited Switzerland with the idea of setting up a watch factory to take advantage of lower wage rates and local expertise. In 1869 Florentine Ariosto Jones from Boston settled in Schaffhausen in eastern Switzerland – an unlikely spot, far from the traditional watchmaking centers of the Jura and Geneva – where he was offered a factory with hydroelectric power from the Rhine. Jones, who had visions of exporting his products back to the U.S.A., called his company the International Watch Co.

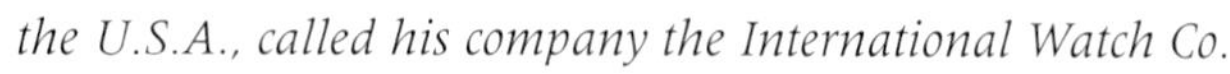

ABOVE
GRANDE COMPLICATION
With nine hands and 659 mechanical parts, a technological masterpiece.

ABOVE
DA VINCI
A gem of a Da Vinci in 18kt gold, with 149 diamonds and 12 rubies on the dial.

The early years were hard, and although production reached 400,000 pieces in 1872 – thanks to the new machines introduced by Jones – sales fell off. His export plan failed because of the high import duty (24%), and by 1875 the firm was in the hands of the bank, which appointed Johan Rauschenbach, a successful local engineer, as Managing Director.

The survival of the company owes much to a talented watchmaker, Urs Haenggi, who joined in 1883 and stayed the rest of his life. He put the company's affairs in order and introduced new calibers to the products. Rauschenbach's son and successor had proved of little help, but his granddaughter Bertha had married Ernst Homberger, a Schaffhausen industrialist, who in 1905 was awarded powers of attorney to act for members of the family, which included Bertha's elder sister and her husband C. G. Jung, the famous psychiatrist.

Ernst Homberger took over the running of the business in 1929 and renamed it Uhrenfabrik Ernst Homberger Rauschenbach; when his father-in-law died, Ernst dropped his name from the title. In the mid-1950s Ernst's son Hans took control; an Anglophile who had rowed at Henley, he renamed it International Watch Co. H E Homberger AG. He was the last private owner. Since 1978, when the Swiss watch industry was in serious trouble and the company was rescued by an injection of capital from VDO, a German industrial conglomerate,

PRODUCT RANGE

Grande Complication
Da Vinci
Novecento
Pilot XII
Ingenieur
Il Destriero Scafusia

IWC

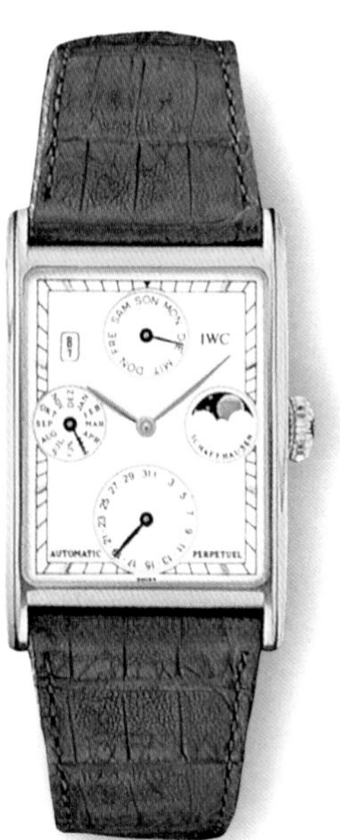

RIGHT
NOVECENTO
The Novecento in 18kt gold with leather strap. The first rectangular watch with a perpetual calendar.

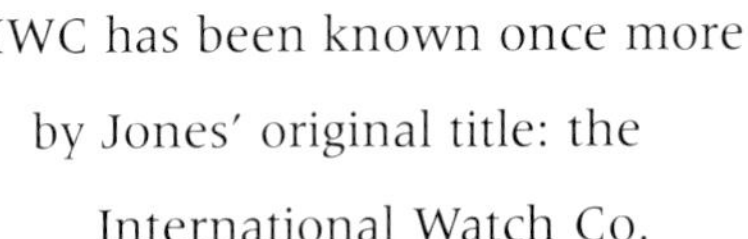

RIGHT
Classic chronograph Rattrapante, with hand-wound chronograph movement and patented split-second mechanism under a domed sapphire crystal glass.

FACT FILE

FOUNDED: 1869
COUNTRY OF ORIGIN: Switzerland
OUTPUT: Information not available
MOVEMENT: Mechanical 80%, quartz 20%
CEO: Hannes A. Pantli

IWC has been known once more by Jones' original title: the International Watch Co.

Since its early days, IWC has made watchmaking history. Jones's original 19 ligne calibers, one of the first to feature crown winding, are collector's treasures. In 1885 the company produced the first-ever pocket watch with digital hour and minute displays. 1890 saw its first Grande Complication, with 1,000 parts that took a year to assemble and finish by hand. IWC was among the first to make wristwatches based on one of their ladies pocket watches, and it supplied marine chronometers to several of the world's navies.

The mid-1930s saw the launch of its first wristwatch designed specially for pilots. Its movement was protected against magnetic fields, a feature which was incorporated into the famous Ingenieur line with its soft iron inner case and ability to withstand 500,000 a/m.

The Portugieser is another re-issue. Created originally as an extra large wristwatch with a pocket watch movement, the split-second chronograph version of 1995 had a hand-wound Cal 76240 movement with 45 hours of power reserve. Later it was made even more complicated by the addition of a minute repeater – now powered by the 952-caliber movement visible through a sapphire case back – in a limited edition of 250 pieces in rose or yellow gold and only 50 in platinum.

BELOW
IWC Portugieser movement. In the late 1930s, the Portugieser series became the first wristwatches to contain high-precision pocket watch movement.

IWC has always had a reputation for complicated watches and in 1985 produced the Da Vinci, which set a new standard for wrist chronographs. It had an automatic mechanical perpetual calendar programmed for 514 years without normal adjustment (leap years included). It had nine hands and four dials and displayed hours, numbers, seconds, elapsed time, and phases of the moon. Ten years later, it was reintroduced with a split-second chronograph – it now had a tenth hand!

The Destriero Scafusia was built in a series of just 125 to mark the company's 125th anniversary. It has a rattrapante chronograph mechanism and a mechanically

ABOVE
For more than 100 years IWC have been using the best tools to produce their watches: their hands.

programed perpetual calendar whose tourbillon and handcrafted decoration are visible through the sapphire case back. It retailed in Britain at £125,000.

ABOVE
Novecento with date window. The first Novecento appeared in 1987, and the rectangular shape is still popular.

IWC and Porsche Design have been working together since 1978, and the collaboration has resulted in a collection of super-sleek, all-black, titanium-cased models with automatic chronograph movements whose push buttons were totally integrated into the case. Some even, remarkably, incorporated a compass – which is, of course, shockproof and water-resistant just like the watch, naturally.

Since its early days, IWC has had to fend for itself; removed from the traditional centers, it had to train its own craftsmen – it is one of the few firms licensed to award a certificate as *"horloger complet."* Quality is still all-important – so important that it is embodied in the company's philosophy and in the legend inscribed on the back of some of its watches – *Probus Scafusia* – a pride of workmanship.

FLAGSHIP LINE

The wartime "Pilot's" watch became in 1948 the celebrated Mark XI, IWC's first megastar, sought by collectors all over the world. Ten years later came the Mark XII. It had an automatic movement and a soft iron core that makes it impervious to magnetic interference. With its black dial and clear white numbers, date display, and slim center seconds hand, it became the flagship of IWC's line. It was available on strap or bracelet, in steel or 18-karat gold; in a ladies' version with a smaller case; and in a style called Fliegerchronograph with split seconds and the customary chronograph functions in a case of zirconium oxide – a high-tech ceramic – with a matte black finish. A final version had all the features of its predecessors, except it was driven by two quartz movements and double stepping motors.

LEFT
MARK XII FLIEGER-CHRONOGRAPH

№26

JAEGER-LECOULTRE

Jaeger-LeCoultre still occupies the same site in the village of Le Sentier in the Vallée de Joux where it was established in 1833 by Charles Antoine LeCoultre. The Jaeger name comes from the company's merger nearly a century later with the watch division of a French marine chronometer maker, Edward Jaeger, who having worked with the firm for 20 years was taken into partnership in 1937.

ABOVE
REVERSO SHADOW
With an authentic, functional look of the 1930s.

ABOVE
REVERSO DUO
Two time indications on back-to-back dials from a single mechanical movement.

Antoine LeCoultre was an inventive man who equipped his workshop with the latest industrial machinery and himself developed a number of innovative pieces of equipment. He is also credited, along with a number of others, with developing a winding and setting mechanism that made the watch key obsolete.

By the end of the century the company was specializing in chronographs, minute repeaters, and alarm watches and in 1903 was making the world's thinnest watch movements in regular production. 1928 saw the development of the Atmos clock, which works indefinitely (up to 600 years, it is claimed) from minute changes in air temperature, and the company's watchmakers followed this by producing what is still the world's smallest mechanical movement; the 98 parts of caliber 101 weigh less than a gram.

But it was in 1931 that Jaeger-LeCoultre produced a watch that was to give it international fame – the Reverso. It was introduced, they say, in response to a demand from some British officers in India for a watch that could withstand the rigors of a game of polo while preserving an appearance worthy of a "sporting gentleman." Their ingenious solution was a watch whose rectangular case flipped over, turning its back on the world to protect the delicate movement.

PRODUCT RANGE

Master Grand Taille
Master Réveil
Master Extra Slim
Master Lady
Master Classic
Master Géographique
Reverso
Reverso Minute Repeater
Reverso Tourbillon
Reverso Chronograph
Reverso Joaillerie
Reverso 101
Reverso Shadow
Reverso Duo

JAEGER-LECOULTRE

RIGHT
MASTER REVEIL
With automatic alarm. Each watch has passed Jaeger-LeCoultre's 1000-hr rating and reliability test.

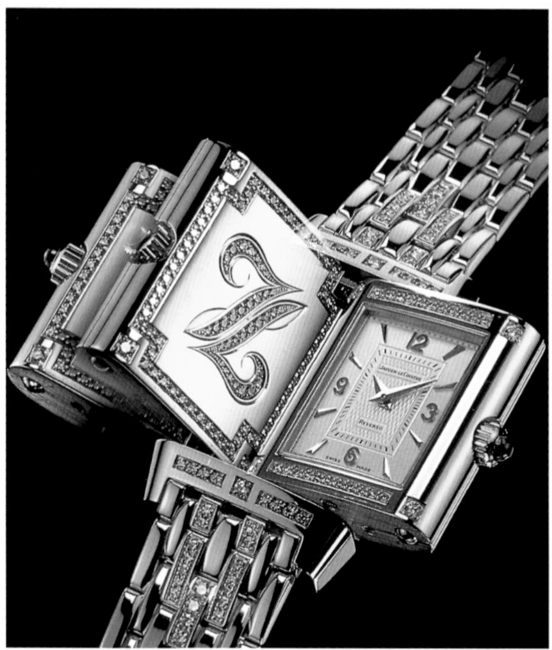

LEFT
Reverso Joaillerie, with detail. Another stunning version, encrusted with diamonds and emeralds.

ABOVE
A beautiful variation on the Reverso theme is this "Joaillerie" version, with the exquisite case and bracelet embedded with diamonds.

Sadly World War II and its aftermath pushed the Reverso into decline, and by the 1970s it had almost disappeared. At the same time, the company was facing the quartz revolution, which had cut down the Swiss watchmaking industry to a fifth of its former size. The German instrument-making firm VDO moved in and took over Jaeger-LeCoultre along with IWC at Schaffhausen and others in Germany and France. One of the latter was Yema, owned by Henri-Jean Belmont, who was subsequently asked in 1986 by the new chairman, Gunter Blümlein, to take on the job of putting Jaeger-LeCoultre back on the map.

FACT FILE

FOUNDED: 1833
COUNTRY OF ORIGIN: Switzerland
OUTPUT: 28,000 watches, 8,000 clocks per annum
MOVEMENT: Mechanical 70%, quartz 30%
CEO: Henri-Jean Belmont

Belmont has five generations of watchmaking skill in his blood and ten years after his appointment heads up a company employing 545 people with a turnover in excess of SF100 million, and an annual production of 28,000 watches and 8,000 alarm clocks. Today it is the biggest employer in the Vallée de Joux.

One of Belmont's first tasks was to reorganize the collection, to weed out unprofitable lines, and to concentrate on what the company did best, which was to make high-quality watches.

BELOW
Detail of the new calibre 960. This took three-and-a-half years of research and 500 technical drawings to perfect.

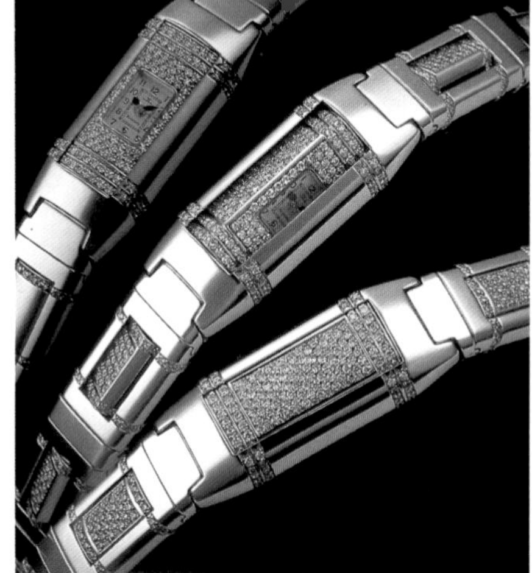

ABOVE
Jaeger-LeCoultre watches provide a perfect combination of complexity, beauty, originality and practicality.

Jaeger-leCoultre now has two basic lines; the Master series is based on a classic design of the 1950s and includes a Grande Taille, with a fast beat automatic movement, a Master Réveil automatic with alarm (an echo of the Memovox, a 1956 model which was the first automatic watch with an alarm), a manually wound Master-Slim, and a Master Lady with a specially created small automatic movement. The latest addition is the Master Géographique, which displays on command the time in major cities of the world. It has two winding crowns, a date display as a subdial, a reserve-power indicator, and the names of the selected cities on a circular display below 6 o'clock.

Its other and more famous line – and now its Flagship – is the Reverso. It still comes in simple form,on a strap or bracelet, in gold or steel. It is available with two time zones (and two faces), with an alarm, and with a minute repeater (created in 1994 and limited world-wide to 500 pieces in 18-karat pink gold and sold on a strap). This was the third complicated version, and it followed the 60th Jubilee model (1991) and the Reverso Tourbillon (1993), both of which were also limited editions. The next year, the company introduced a Reverso Chronograph Retrograde, which displays the normal features of timekeeping on one face with the back reserved for chronograph functions.

The Reverso Joaillerie was bedecked with diamonds on the rectangular bezel of its 18-karat gold case and the links of its delicate bracelet. But the triumph of the company's master jewelers came in 1996 with the launch of the Reverso 101. The world's smallest mechanical movement was squeezed into a rectangular case which pivots to reveal a diamond-encrusted back; more diamonds embellish the shoulders and sides, while the matching gold bracelet has pivoting center panels which turn to reveal a double row of diamonds or a plain polished surface. It comes in yellow, pink, or white gold.

BELOW
REVERSO CHRONOGRAPH

FLAGSHIP LINE

The Flagship is undoubtedly the Reverso in all its forms, from simple gold case on strap to diamond-studded mini-versions. The line now accounts for 60 percent of the firm's total turnover.

JEAN LASSALE

In 1975 a meeting between a Swiss watchmaker and a French entrepreneur led to the founding of a company in Geneva under the name Jean Lassale. The watchmaker specialized in ultraslim mechanical movements – only 1.2mm thick – housed in beautifully turned and decorated cases which the company claimed at its launch were the slimmest in the world.

PRODUCT RANGE

Thalassa Classics
Thalassa 200 Divers
Thalassa Chronograph
Thalassa Five Star
Gents Dress

JEAN LASSALE

In the early 1980s, the company was acquired by the Seiko Group, who had produced the first commercially viable quartz watch and was very involved in the new electronic technology. It was natural that the company should associate its slim quartz movements with the Jean Lassale brand. The single brand name "Lassale" was used for a selection of gold-plated dress watches from Japan, while the full "Jean Lassale" name is reserved exclusively for Swiss-made watches cased in gold and stainless steel. Some of the cases, bracelets, and even dials were studded with high-quality precious stones.

In 1985 Jean Lassale's Thalassa range won the European Golden Laurel award for design and technical quality, which the company also won in 1991 for its Star collection. Both lines featured the distinctive "porthole" profile created by Swiss designer Jorg Hysek. The same profile also appears in the Caribbean and Les Classics models of more recent years.

The company is a firm believer in two-way communication between its customers and itself. To that end, it has introduced the concept of the personalized timepiece. Recognizing that clients

RIGHT
GENTS DRESS
"Skeleton" model, showing traditional mechanical movements.

LEFT
THALASSA 200 DIVER'S
Stainless steel with quartz movement. Water-resistant to 660ft.

BELOW
THALASSA
Chronograph, with steel and yellow metal case and crocodile strap. Unusual glass back.

FACT FILE

FOUNDED: 1975
COUNTRY OF ORIGIN: Switzerland
OUTPUT: Information not available
MOVEMENT: Mechanical and quartz
CEO: Ian D. Shaw

are highly individualistic people with their own ideas of taste and lifestyle, the company offers a "bespoke" option on all its models. Under the title Special Watches for Special People, owners are encouraged to suggest their own choice of dial finish, stone setting, straps, or bracelets. Gold dials in 18-, 22-, or even 24-karat are hand engraved to the customer's requirements, and the company quotes such distinguished clients as Sir Peter Ustinov, Gina Lollobrigida, and Roy Lichtenstein among its Special People.

In spite of being wholly owned by a Japanese watch group, Jean Lassale watches, of whatever design, are Swiss-made. That means that more than half the cost of manufacture of the movement, crown, hands, and dial has been incurred in Switzerland and that the watch has been cased and tested in Switzerland by qualified watchmakers. The company makes the point that all cases, bracelets, and associated components are sourced in Switzerland with the sole exception of their Louisiana-farmed crocodile skins and Conolly hide leather straps.

The movements in Jean Lassale watches, whether quartz or mechanical, are also Swiss-made and are so engraved. Their chronometer models carry the certificate of the Swiss Official Chronometer Testing Authority (COSC).

ABOVE
Thalassa Eclat, polished execution with unique "hourglass" band.

The Thalassa collection is still Jean Lassale's flagship line. Its distinctive "porthole" case is available in two sizes, in 18-karat gold, gold and steel, or all steel. It can be set with diamonds on request. It has a Swiss quartz movement, a scratch-resistant crystal, and is water-resistant to 100 feet. Bracelets to match the case are offered in a choice of designs. The Thalassa 200 is a diver's watch with a water resistance of 660 feet; it has a quartz movement, with center seconds hand and date window; the case has a rotating bezel. The Chronograph has a quartz movement with four micromotors; it displays hours, minutes, seconds, and date; the flyback hand measures to 5/100ths of a second; and the model is available in the customary three executions, on strap or bracelet. At the top of the line is the Thalassa Five Star, which has a multifunction quartz movement and an analogical display indicating day, date, second time zone, and moonphase. It is available in steel, gold and steel, or all 18-karat gold. It has a scratch-resistant sapphire crystal and is water-resistant to 100 feet.

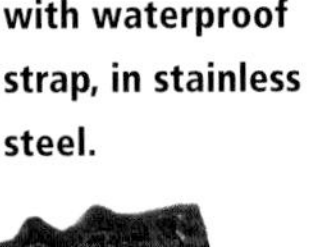

BELOW
THALASSA
Classic Thalassa, with waterproof strap, in stainless steel.

FLAGSHIP LINE

The Thalassa Collection in all its forms is Jean Lassale's flagship line.

№28

Junghans

Junghans Mega Solar Ceramic is undoubtedly one of the most advanced timepieces created since people first started telling the time 5,000 years ago.

Junghans, established at Schramberg in the Black Forest 135 years ago, was Germany's largest producer of clocks. The company first developed a radio-controlled mantel clock in 1985, and by 1990 had reduced it to wristwatch size in a digital model called Mega I, quickly followed the next year by an analog version. 1992 saw a lady's model, and 1993 the first of the solar-powered watches, the Mega Solar, still radio-controlled, with the antenna in the bracelet and taking its energy from the sun. The latest development is the Mega Solar Ceramic with the antenna housed in its high-tech case.

RIGHT

MEGA

Picks up time signal from Frankfurt once a day. Has automatic time setting for summer/winter.

ABOVE

MEGA STAR

Radio-controlled watch with three hands and stopwatch feature.

There are four main lines in Junghans' selection of watches. Mega Solar Ceramic is a radio-controlled watch in a ceramic case that is virtually indestructible. Made from zirconium oxide and produced under high pressure at a temperature of 3600°F (2000°C), it is heat resistant, scratchproof, harder than stainless steel, and resistant to chemicals. It is also kind to the skin and very light; since it does not act as a barrier to radio signals, the very sensitive antenna can be housed within it. The movement draws its energy from light, while its energy store can provide a power reserve to power the watch for six months. If it is left in darkness for longer, it can be reactivated by light in just a matter of moments; then without any further adjustment by the wearer, it will automatically set itself to the right time.

PRODUCT RANGE

Mega Solar Ceramic
Mega Ceramic
Mega Star
Solar Tec
Wall, mantel, and alarm clocks

JUNGHANS

LEFT

MEGA

Another example from the line. Here the PVD coated steel case is colored anthracite.

LEFT
Junghans Solar TEC – a new generation of solar wristwatches.

The secret is its reception of radio signals from one of the universal time stations, with one of which it is in constant radio contact. The signals automatically set the time, change from summer to winter time, and make time zone adjustments for the world traveler. It has a transmitter call-up button and internal time memory. The matte-blasted anthracite case has an analog dial, a date window at 6 o'clock, and is water-resistant to 100 feet.

The Mega Ceramic offers the same high-tech radio-controlled timekeeping, the same diamond-hard ceramic case, and has in addition a stopwatch function. It has a stainless steel bracelet and is water-resistant to 100 feet.

The Mega Star is another radio-controlled line with date, center seconds hand, and stopwatch feature in a high-fashion plastic case on a strap or flexible bracelet, aimed specifically at young technically orientated people, and priced accordingly.

Solar Tec is a new sporty line in PVD or palladium-coated cases in modern designs. New technology has allowed Junghans to design much smaller solar wristwatches with slender female wrists in mind. The cases have mineral glasses and are water-resistant to 100 feet. The man's Solar Tec model has a seconds hand, mechanical date, and charge level indicator in a water-resistant palladium-plated case with matching matte-blasted bracelet. It has a power reserve of two months.

With its mantel and alarm clock models, Junghans has about 20 percent of Germany's market for watches and clocks.

BELOW
MEGA SOLAR CERAMIC

FACT FILE

FOUNDED: 1861
COUNTRY OF ORIGIN: Germany
OUTPUT: 80,000 watches, clocks, and movements per day
MOVEMENT: Solar, quartz, and radio-controlled
CEO: Wolfgang Fritz

FLAGSHIP LINE

Junghans Mega Solar Ceramic.

LONGINES

In 1832 Auguste Aggassiz set up his business in St. Imier in the Jura Mountains. It was a trading house; it consisted of a purchasing office which bought in watch parts, which were then assembled at home by outworkers; a workshop, where the assembled watches were finished and adjusted; and a sales office consisting of Aggassiz himself, who, having organized the work and found the finance, took to the road to sell the finished products.

He stood the rigors of this demanding life for twenty years before finding a successor in his nephew Ernest Francillon. Scion of a banking family in Lausanne, Ernest proved a natural entrepreneur and soon realized that to achieve consistent quality he had to bring all the operations under one roof. In 1867 he opened a plant on the banks of the River Suza on a spot known locally as "Les Longines" – the long meadows – and the firm takes its foundation from that time.

LEFT
FLAGSHIP
Gold plated, water-resistant to 100ft, with sapphire glass.

Where Aggassiz had sold his watches to other houses, Francillon's policy was to sell under his own brand. He named them "Longines" after the factory site and the same year exhibited a pocket hunter that not only earned a commendation at the Paris Exposition, but was the forerunner of a model chosen to be replicated for the firm's 125th anniversary.

ABOVE
GRANDE CLASSIQUE
Gents ultra slim, gold-plated watch, water-resistant to 100ft.

BELOW
NAVIGATOR
Navigator all steel "date" automatic, with mineral glass, water-resistant to 100ft.

Longines' high reputation brought imitators, and in 1889 Francillon had to design and register a trademark to deter them – it was the famous winged hourglass. Quite early in its history, the company became involved in sports timing; its first appearance was at the reborn Olympic Games in Athens in 1896 – an association that has lasted until the present time.

By the 1920s the factory employed 2,500 people, and among its lines of high-grade timepieces was a pocket-watch chronometer mounted in gimbals which became a marine chronometer. Then occurred one of those events which project a company into the international limelight.

PRODUCT RANGE

Conquest VHP
Flagship
Gold Collection
Grande Classique
Navigator
Golden Wings

ABOVE
An elegant watch, in 9kt gold with full diamond bezel.

Charles Lindbergh made the world's first solo crossing of the Atlantic in his monoplane, the *Spirit of St. Louis,* navigating by means of his Longines wristwatch. During the 33-hour flight, he kept himself awake by designing a timepiece which would make it easier for pilots to establish their longitude. His sketch was the basis for Longines' Lindbergh hour Angle watch, which appeared in 1937 and was an instant success.

The company had maintained its interest in sports timing and in 1952 was appointed official timekeeper to the Oslo Olympic Games. But like many companies, to survive the onset of quartz it had to amalgamate, and what had been a family firm for well over a century became part of the General Watch Co., later taken over by ASUAG and subsequently merged into the giant SMH.

Such resources enhanced Longines' ability to produce high-quality watches with both quartz and mechanical movements.

FACT FILE

FOUNDED: 1867
COUNTRY OF ORIGIN: Switzerland
OUTPUT: Information not available
MOVEMENT: Mainly quartz
CEO: Walter von Kaenel

Among the mechanical models was an automatic with twin mainspring barrels; the Cal L990 was claimed to be the thinnest watch with sweep seconds and date ever made. Two years later, the quartz division produced the Feuille d'Or, a leaf of gold, a mere 1.8mm thick – two thirds of a matchstick – by integrating the movement into the gold case back. Then came the first of Longines' Conquest collections of super-accurate quartz watches which was to become the firm's leading line.

An interesting commemorative model – much prized by collectors – was the Cristobal C Collection, launched in 1992 to mark Columbus's voyage to America in 1492 and which contained a solar compass. The same year saw the re-issue of the 1867 hunter pocket watch to mark the company's 125th anniversary.

Longines' current iines include the Gold collection, in 18-karat gold on bracelet or strap for men and women; a collection of 9-karat gold ladies' watches with diamond-set bezels; and another ladies' collection of gold-plated models with a variety of bracelet designs. Most of the cases and dials are of conventional design. Les Grandes Classiques have more delicate gold-plated cases in a very slim execution, with classical dials and Roman numerals. There is a line actually called Flagship, with gold-plated or bicolor cases on close-linked bracelets. All have quartz movements.

BELOW
Golden Wings come in a variety of combinations – not just gold.

RIGHT
Conquest – gents steel and gold plated.

RIGHT
Golden Wings – gents bi-metal on bracelet.

LEFT
Classique – gents gold plated.

But the undoubted star of the collection is the Conquest VHP. VHP stands for Very High Precision, and Longines claims an accuracy of ± 12 seconds a year. The quartz movements are housed in 18-karat gold water-resistant cases in two sizes and are available on strap or bracelet. Conquest VHP watches come complete with an end-of-life battery indicator and a time zone corrector; and the line also includes a multifunction model and a perpetual calendar programed right up to February 28, 2100. Handsome Two-tone models in steel or titanium and gold are also available.

There is a small line of mechanical automatic watches called the Navigator collection, which have day or day date, and are available in steel or steel and gold, with turning bezels on strap or bracelet.

BELOW
CONQUEST VHP PERPETUAL CALENDAR

Perhaps to overcome the somewhat staid appearance of its main collections, Longines has launched a Golden Wings line named after its famous Winged Hourglass trademark. Aimed at a younger market, it consists of a selection of ladies' and men's models in steel, steel and gold, or all gold on an ostrich strap or bracelet; the case design is quite modern, the movements are quartz, and some models have diamond-set bezels. A top-of-the-market collection.

FLAGSHIP LINE

The Conquest VHP, first launched in 1984, with an accuracy that was claimed to be five times more precise than ordinary quartz watches, has been Longines' most successful line. Over the years it has acquired an Admirals' model, a Columbus commemoration, and a perpetual calendar. The final version is the Conquest Chronograph.

№30

Maurice Lacroix

Maurice Lacroix was founded just 20 years ago in Sainelegier in the Jura, but in that short time it has acquired a quite outstanding reputation – in fact, it is said to be the second-largest selling Swiss watch in Germany after Rolex.

ABOVE

LES MECHANIQUES

Chronograph with high quality movement, with high-grade steel case and leather strap.

Maurice Lacroix is part of the Desco Group, a leading distributor of Swiss watch brands throughout the Far and Middle East. After much experience in private label watches, Desco launched Maurice Lacroix in 1975.

The movements of its watches range from ETA quartz to mechanical Complications. It is particularly noted for its blend of style with quality at competitive prices, emphasized by its link with dress designer Amanda Wakeley, whose clothes, it believes, share the same characteristics of understated glamor and care over details as Maurice Lacroix watches.

The current Maurice Lacroix line contains about 100 models, and these have been divided into a number of collections.

Fabia, formerly Les Classiques, is a wide collection of styles in two sizes, round or rectangular, in steel or gold-plated cases, and modestly water-resistant, on straps or bracelets with quartz movements.

ABOVE

LES CLASSIQUES

This classically elegant watch is water-resistant to 100ft.

RIGHT

CALYPSO

Inspired by the Calypso, a ship owned by Jacques-Yves Cousteau.

Calypso comes in four sizes with quartz or mechanical movements on leather straps or metal bracelets, in cases of steel, bicolor steel, and 18-karat gold plate, gold plated, steel and 18-karat gold or solid 18-karat gold, water-resistant to 330 feet, with sapphire crystal and screwdown crown. The latest model is the Tiago, whose slim stainless-steel case comes in two sizes; the Arabic numerals are tritium coated and give the models a unique appearance (Maurice Lacroix is renowned for the variety and quality of its dials). The screwdown crown and sapphire crystal provide water-resistance to 330 feet. The quartz movement has a battery with an end-of-life indicator.

PRODUCT RANGE

Fabia
Calypso
Les Mechaniques
Masterpiece Collection
Les Classiques

Maurice Lacroix

RIGHT

Tiago – the latest model in the Calypso series. The slim stainless steel case comes in two sizes.

Les Mechaniques, as its name implies, is a collection of models with mechanical movements from simple handwound to complicated self-winding chronographs. The cases are steel or 18-karat gold plate and have sapphire crystals front and back; they are water-resistant to 100 feet and are fitted with rather fine leather straps – another ML specialty – or chunky bracelets.

At the top of the Mechaniques line is the Masterpiece Collection, which includes a number of specialties in the mechanical watch field. One is the Jumping Hour model with its single minute hand, small seconds at 6 o'clock, and hour opening just below 12 o'clock. The line includes a ladies' automatic and a host of automatic chronographs with a variety of dials and functions. Newly released is the Venus Chronograph in a solid platinum case housing a complicated chronograph hand-decorated movement, with crown and push pieces of 18-karat white gold; the richly engraved sterling silver dial sets off the 18-karat rose gold hands. Only 125 of these collectors' timepieces have been produced.

FACT FILE

FOUNDED: 1975
COUNTRY OF ORIGIN: Switzerland
OUTPUT: Information not available
MOVEMENT: Mechanical and quartz
CEO: Christian Wehli

LEFT

Venus is a newly released chronograph in a solid platinum case.

RIGHT

CALYPSO
Ladies 18kt gold with diamonds in-set on dial and bezel.

FLAGSHIP LINE

Calypso, with its many alternatives, is Maurice Lacroix's most popular line, especially the round-cased model in steel and 18-karat gold plate on matching bracelet.

№31

Michel Herbelin

Fifty years ago, a talented young French watchmaker named Michel Herbelin opened a workshop in Charquemont, in the Jura Mountains just across the border from Switzerland. To start with he assembled private-label watches for other companies, concentrating particularly on the quality of his manufacture. He soon gained a reputation not only for the reliability and quality of his products, but also for their esthetic appeal. But he aspired to have his own brand, and in 1968 he launched his first collection under the name Michel Herbelin.

In the early 1970s, under the direction of his elder son Jean-Claude, the brand began to acquire an international reputation. The introduction of modern production methods allowed the company to expand, and soon more than 60 percent of the factory's output was sent for export. The majority of sales are to the Middle and Far East, although the brand has a respectable clientele in Europe. In France it has had real success and is now the leading independent watchmaker, with 12 percent of the market in its price field.

Michel Herbelin himself retired from active participation in 1995, and the business, although a limited company, is run virtually as a family concern by his two sons Jean-Claude and Pierre-Michel. At present it employs 90 personnel and produces around 150,000 pieces annually, of which 90 percent are quartz.

The Michel Herbelin line is noted for the softness of its contours, its harmonious dimensions, and its subtle details. The design team works under the close personal direction of Jean-Claude Herbelin and produces two collections a year.

The current collection contains three main lines.

A Classics line, designed for day wear, has a traditional shape, Swiss mechanical handwound and automatic movements, and finely crafted dials.

PRODUCT RANGE

Newport
Classics
Sports
Dress
Safari
Cables

Michel Herbelin

ABOVE
CABLES
Unusual watch with stainless steel ionised cables.

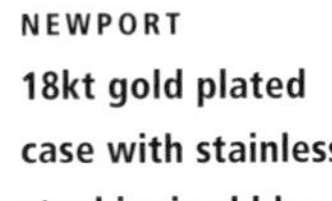

RIGHT
NEWPORT
18kt gold plated case with stainless steel ionised blue titanium-plated bezel.

RIGHT
LADIES CLASSIC
Palladium plated case and bracelet. Scratch-proof sapphire crystal, water-resistant to 100ft, Swiss quartz movement.

A Sports line is epitomized by Newport, the company's Flagship collection, and Safari. The line includes chronographs as well as normal timekeepers. Typical is the round Newport in 18-karat gold and ionized blue stainless-steel case and matching bracelet. It has a screwdown crown, sapphire glass, is water-resistant to 165 feet, and has a Swiss quartz movement. An alternative Newport design has a softly rounded square case in His and Hers models, in stainless steel and 18-karat gold-plated water-protected cases on sharkskin straps.

RIGHT
The beautiful, elegant lines of this Michel Herbelin watch are complemented by a mother-of-pearl dial.

A Dress line in 18-karat gold-plated cases is available on straps or bracelets in bicolor and 18-karat gold-plated or palladium plate. Cables is an elegant round design in 18-karat gold plate with a stainless-steel ionized blue titanium-plated cable bracelet. It has a Swiss quartz movement.

FACT FILE

FOUNDED: 1946
COUNTRY OF ORIGIN: France
OUTPUT: 150,000 units per annum
MOVEMENT: Quartz 95%, mechanical 5%
CEO: Jean-Claude Herbelin

BELOW
NEWPORT
With rectangular case, round corners.

An unusual design is Corynthe from the Classics line plated in white precious metal, with a bezel of concentric rings and matching bracelet. It has a mother-of-pearl dial and a Swiss quartz movement.

The majority of the movements are Swiss ETA Flatline Quartz, with the Valjou 7750 automatic chronograph movement in the complicated models like the Safari.

Quartz movements from France Ebauches, France's largest manufacturer, are also used. Great emphasis is put on quality control, and every watch is finished by hand.

FLAGSHIP LINE

The Newport line, especially the rectangular cases with rounded corners introduced in 1995. They have Swiss quartz movements and sapphire crystals, screwdown crowns, and are water resistant to 165 feet.

№32

MOVADO

A young watchmaker named Achille Ditesheim established a watch manufacturing company with just six workers in La Chaux de Fonds in 18981. By 1889 he had 80 employees, and his chronometers were awarded their first official certificates. The following year the company received a silver medal at the Universal Exhibition in Paris.

ABOVE

MUSEUM "LA NOUVELLE"

Quartz movement, curved case with sapphire glass.

In 1905 the company Ditesheim et Frères changed its name to Movado, an Esperanto word meaning "always in motion." The factory was now capable of large-scale production, and adopted a trademark – a hand holding a pocket watch.

For the next five years, Movado introduced a number of precision calibers and over 700 different case designs, among which was the Polyplan, in an elongated rectangular shape with a movement on three levels. It was the first wristwatch to follow the curve of the wrist, and by now – 1912 – half of all Movado's models were wristwatches.

ABOVE

SUNWATCH

Simplicity, elegance and functionality are combined in this Bauhaus-inspired watch.

In 1926 Movado introduced the Ermeto. Forerunner of today's travel clock, it had an "automatic" winding movement activated by opening and closing the case cover. It is said that an early model was presented to Albert Einstein; certainly it is a highly sought collector's piece.

The 1930s were a period of intense development for the company. It produced the first rectangular mechanical wristwatch with digital display, a double-button chronograph, and an early water-resistant model, the Acvatic. It received more than 1,500 awards and gained a reputation for innovation.

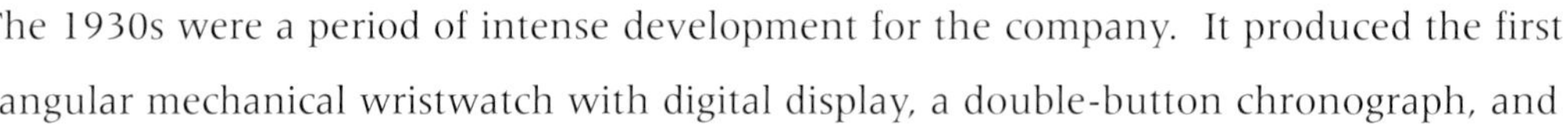

PRODUCT RANGE

Museum Watch
Vizio
Black Sapphire
Museum Classic
Sunwatch
1881 Rectangulaire

MOVADO

In 1961 Movado introduced the Museum Watch, the creation of an American designer, Nathan George Horwitt. He had an obsession about clutter, and had designed and patented an unsuccessful digital clock. In 1947 he produced a matte black dial with a gold dot at 12 o'clock (symbolizing the sun) in a classic gold case. In 1959 the Museum of Modern Art in New York accepted Nathan's watch as a permanent exhibit. He then hawked his prototype around 15 US watch factories. Only Movado, looking for an unusual design to exemplify the founder's desire for innovation, were interested. But the Museum Watch was not enough to make the company's fortunes, and in 1969

RIGHT

CALENDOMATIC

Steel and yellow metal case, leather strap and automatic movement.

ABOVE
1881 gold rectangular watch. Movado has received 1,500 international awards for watch designs and time measuring technology since the company was founded.

Movado was acquired, along with Mondia, by the Zenith Watch Co., which was eventually acquired by a Swiss businessman. In 1983 Movado was taken over by the North American Watch Corporation and almost immediately the influence of a marketing-orientated organization became apparent. Over the next four years, turnover increased twenty-fold; Movado was introduced to new markets in over 60 countries. The Museum watch played a significant part, and in its classic form it is still the company's flagship model.

In 1988 Movado invented the first "art" watch, designed by Andy Warhol. "Times/5" was produced in a limited edition of 250 pieces and inaugurated Movado's Artist Series of watches, which subsequently included models designed by pop artist Yaacov Agam, sculptor Arman, James A. Rosenquist, and the Swiss artist Max Bill.

In 1990 Movado switched its allegiance to sports with the sponsorship of Pete Sampras on the international tennis circuit, and later formed the Movado Children's Foundation to aid children's charities through the sale of the Artist Series.

FACT FILE

FOUNDED: 1881
COUNTRY OF ORIGIN: Switzerland
OUTPUT: Information not available
MOVEMENT: Mechanical and quartz
CEO: Kurt Burki

Horwitt's original concept explicitly used the sun in the shape of a gold dot as the focal point of the dial. With a fine irony, in 1995 Movado launched the Sunwatch, a solar-powered Museum watch. For 1996 Movado introduced Vizio, another Esperanto-inspired title (it means vision) and the North American Watch Corporation – still Movado's owner – changed its name to Movado Group Inc. In celebration, the company produced a book, *The History of Movado*, which outlines its distinguished past.

Movado also produces a number of other models of more conventional design, including an automatic model with a perpetual calendar with moonphase, a rectangular manually wound watch in 18-karat gold case, a chronograph with tachymeter in steel or steel with gold inlays, an automatic with power reserve display, and an automatic chronometer with a COSC certificate. There is a diver's model, water-resistant to 1,000 feet, and the 1881 Basic line with automatic movement, center seconds, and pointer date in stainless steel on strap or bracelet.

FLAGSHIP LINE

The Museum Classic Line has been Movado's flagship since its inception in 1961; it has remained almost unchanged, its movement varying from slim quartz to the solar-powered Sunwatch.

BELOW
MUSEUM CLASSIC
Almost unchanged in 30 years.

№33

Franck Muller

Franck Muller first started to develop his own designs in 1983, although he did not establish his own company until 1991. Having graduated from the celebrated watchmaker's school in Geneva, his hometown, at first he designed watches for collectors and connoisseurs, but then began to make exclusive timepieces of his own design.

In 1986 he produced a Free-Oscillation Tourbillon wristwatch with jumping hours and a regulator-type dial which incorporated a complication he had been working on since 1983. It has a handwound mechanical movement.

In 1987 he added a minute repeater to his free-oscillation tourbillon, which could be seen through an opening in the case back. Only one unique piece – now owned by a private collector – was ever made.

In 1989 a Perpetual Calendar joined the Minute Repeater in a watch with an inverted tourbillon. It took two years to develop and build his exceptional piece, which contains several hundred parts.

In 1992 Franck Muller produced his most complicated watch, which had Grande and Petite strike; minute repeater at hours, quarters, and minutes; perpetual calendar programed to 2100 with day date mark and monthly equation of time; moonphase; 24-hour indicator; and thermometer. It was cased in platinum, and the movement was manually wound.

The next year saw the introduction of Calibre 93 which contained several Grande Complications including a split-second chronograph. Also in 1993 he introduced a further refinement to the Minute Repeater – the striking indicator. The invention, which he has patented, allows the movement of the minute track to be displayed by means of a retrograde hand on the dial.

PRODUCT RANGE

Tourbillon
Minute Repeater
Perpetual Calendar
Grande Sonnerie
Calibre 93
Calibre 95
Endurance 24
Master Calendar
Casablanca

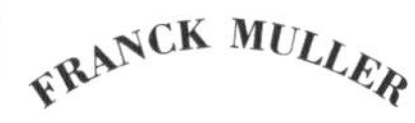

ABOVE
LADIES MINI-TONNEAU
18kt white gold curved case and bracelet, with single row of diamonds around the bezel. Mechanical movement.

LEFT
JUMPING HOUR REGULATOR
With Cintrée Curvex case in 18kt pink gold and crocodile strap. The hour shows in aperture and dial has "sunburst effect".

RIGHT
CASABLANCA
A distinctive shape, here with a salmon dial. It has luminous hands and mechanical automatic movement.

ABOVE
The Frank Muller collection offers a dazzling array of forms and complications. From left to right: Calibre 95; the distinctive curved cintrée case; chronograph.

His inventions were often housed in cases with curved rectangular sides, which he christened Cintrée Curvex. Typical of these is the 2852 Regulator, or the 7500 with Thirties-style dial and small seconds, or the Casablanca with its stark black dial.

A typical example of his super complications is Calibre 95 which contains a tourbillon, split-second chronograph, perpetual calendar, indication of leap years, 24-hour meter, moonphases, and temperature of the mechanism.

This unique watch offers two magnificent watches in the same creation. It is double-sided – the day dial is silvered and indicates the horological complications. The night side is set with Top Wessellton diamonds in a platinum case which displays the skeleton movement and a pair of hands which just tell the time in hours and minutes.

Franck Muller is a regular exhibitor at the International Salon of Haute Horlogerie, which takes place in Geneva every spring. Each year he has launched an exceptional piece – each a new world première. For 1996 it was a Tourbillon with minute repeater with retrograde striking indicator in a gold Cintrée Curvex case.

FACT FILE

FOUNDED: 1991
COUNTRY OF ORIGIN: Switzerland
OUTPUT: Limited editions
MOVEMENT: Mechanical and quartz
CEO: Franck Muller

He also launched Endurance 24, in which the dial indicates the time over 24 hours instead of the normal 12. It is a mechanical chronograph with manual winding, in a limited series of 250 pieces in steel, 50 pieces in 18-karat gold, and 50 in platinum. The watch was created in conjunction with McLaren, whose new racing car will carry Franck Muller's name, and in tribute to two of motor racing's renowned events, LeMans and the Daytona 24-hour races, in the BPR Championship calendar.

BELOW
REGULATOR
With classic Cintrée curved case.

FLAGSHIP LINE

Since Franck Muller's creations are usually individual pieces, or in limited editions, there is no Flagship line – Muller himself says that each watch has a personality of its own. His hallmark is probably the curved Cintrée case.

№34

OMEGA

When, in 1969, Neil Armstrong made his first "giant leap for mankind," he also gave a hefty boost to one of Switzerland's best-known watch brands. The watch itself was a handwound mechanical chronograph and by today's standards was a pretty conventional model. So why had NASA selected Omega as the official timekeeper for its astronauts?

ABOVE

DE VILLE
18kt gold case, crocodile strap. Chronometer certified and water-resistant to 100ft.

When Louis Brandt, descendant of a watchmaking family, set up shop in the already well-known town of La Chaux de Fonds, he produced keywound pocket watches in silver. In 1877 he registered his company as Louis Brandt et Fils; two years later he died, and Louis-Paul and his younger brother César moved the business to Bienne where there was a greater supply of labor.

The original workshop had been a *comptoir d'établissage* in which movements and parts bought from specialist houses were assembled by home workers and then tested before being sold. The brothers abandoned this traditional system in favor of pure manufacture, and the new organization became one of the largest factories in Switzerland, producing around 100,000 watches a year.

By the end of the century, it was making a 13-ligne wristwatch model with striking mechanism – and the name Omega had appeared for the first time on a watch. The story goes that they told their bank manager that their watches were the last word in watchmaking, and he suggested Omega, the last letter in the Greek alphabet and traditional symbol of the ultimate achievement. The company name was changed to Louis Brandt et Frères – Omega Watch Co.

In 1903 control of the company passed to Louis's grandson Paul-Emile, whose influence over the company was to last for the next fifty years. New designs were introduced, and Omega won numerous awards from Observatories around the world in addition to being appointed official timekeeper to 21 Olympic Games.

PRODUCT RANGE
Constellation
Seamaster
Professional
Speedmaster
de Ville

BELOW

SEAMASTER PROFESSIONAL
Chronograph with helium escape valve at 10 o'clock position on case. Chronometer certified.

BELOW

SPEEDMASTER
Moon watch with steel case and strap and mechanical movement – the first watch on the moon.

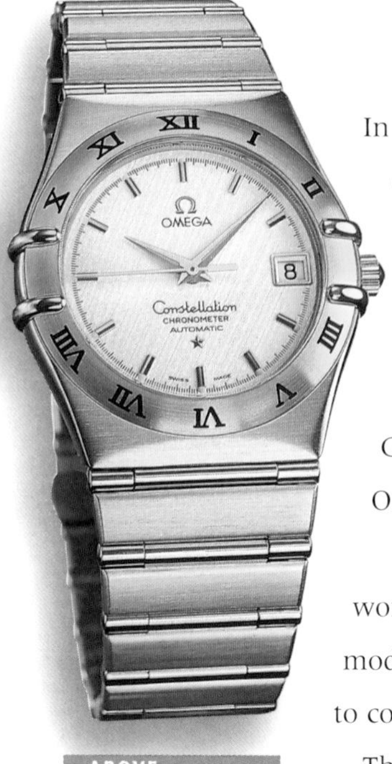

ABOVE
A combination of beauty and precision – the Constellation chronometer automatic.

In 1948 the Omega Seamaster was launched to mark the firm's centenary; four years later came an automatic chronometer called the Constellation, the most successful line for years to come. The firm also introduced a series of ladies' models, such as the Ladymatic. Omega also produced an uninterrupted series of 20,000 automatic Constellation movements, all of which obtained the coveted chronometer certificate of COSC, the official chronograph testing authority. Virgil Grissom wore a Speedmaster in Gemini 3 in August 1965; the famous Moonwalk followed, and when the Russians selected Omega for their Soyuz crew in 1975, Omega was confirmed as the space-age watch.

It would not be too much to say that Omega is synonymous in the minds of many of the world's public with Swiss watches. The company has developed both quartz and mechanical models in a vast range for men and women, from classical dress watches and gemset creations to complicated chronographs and chronometers for specialist purposes.

The Constellation is Omega's most popular and publicized brand. Named for a group of stars, it is available as a man's automatic with chronometer certificate and quartz movement, and as a lady's automatic, quartz, or small quartz. All are available in 18-karat gold, steel and 18-karat gold, or all steel on matching bracelets, are water-resistant to 165 feet in men's sizes and 100 feet in ladies sizes, and have scratch-resistant sapphire crystals.

Seamaster Professional is a line of rugged traditional chronographs for adventurous men; it comes with officially rated mechanical chronometer or quartz movements in titanium or bicolor cases with chunky bracelets and is water-resistant to 1,000 feet. Scratch-resistant sapphire crystals protect the blue dials with their large luminous hour markers.

There are less rugged models with 18-karat gold or stainless-steel cases, water resistant to 400 feet, in two sizes, for those less inclined to plumb the depths.

BELOW
CONSTELLATION (GEMSET)

The Speedmaster, Moonwalk's successor, is available in stainless steel, or 18-karat gold with a handwound movement or as an automatic chronograph. Some ladies versions have diamond-set bezels. All Speedmaster models have mechanical movements.

The de Ville collection is characterized by slim cases in 18-karat gold or stainless-steel and gold bicolor, on fine leather straps or intricately linked bracelets. They are essentially dress watches for special occasions, the movements a choice of quartz, handwound, or self-winding.

FLAGSHIP LINE

The Constellation is Omega's Flagship line, heir to a long tradition of precision records.

FACT FILE

FOUNDED: 1848
COUNTRY OF ORIGIN: Switzerland
OUTPUT: Information not available
MOVEMENT: Mechanical and quartz
CEO: Nicholas Hayek

ORIS

Oris has always been a company with more than a hint of independence. It is typical that its history begins, not in one of the traditional centers of watchmaking, but right at the other end of the Jura Mountains, in the little village of Holstein a few miles south of the industrial region of Basel.

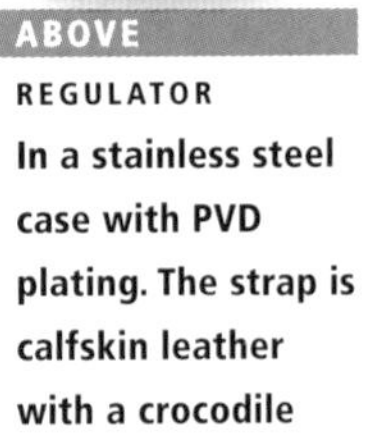

ABOVE

REGULATOR

In a stainless steel case with PVD plating. The strap is calfskin leather with a crocodile pattern.

Paul Cattin and Georges Christian set up a watch factory in 1904 and in a relatively short time it was turning out movement parts as well as cases and dials.

Later they started to make complete watches and in 1938 produced a Pointer Calendar model which has been a feature of the Oris collection ever since. Just before that time, the Swiss government enacted a number of laws to regulate the production of watches. Pin-lever watches did not then enjoy the reputation they subsequently attained, and among the sixty million pin-lever watches produced, undoubtedly some were inferior. Oris, a major producer of pin-lever watches, found itself prohibited from making jeweled lever models as well as certain forms of shock-resist systems allied to jeweled levers.

Oris strove constantly to improve the quality and precision of its watches, which by then were acquiring an international reputation. To demonstrate that pin-lever watches could, if properly made, be accurate, the company entered some of its models in official timing trials at Neuchâtel Observatory, and Oris was awarded an official certificate entitling it to call its watches "chronometers."

To meet the challenge of the electronic revolution, Oris joined Longines, Rado, and others to form General Watch, which was later absorbed into the government-sponsored ASUAG group. When ASUAG later merged with SSIH to join SMH (Societé Suisse de Microélectronique et d'Horlogerie), Oris, independent as ever, decided to get out and in a management buyout became once more a privately owned company.

ABOVE

RECTANGULAR CLASSIC

With stainless steel, PVD plated case, luminous hands and crocodile leather strap.

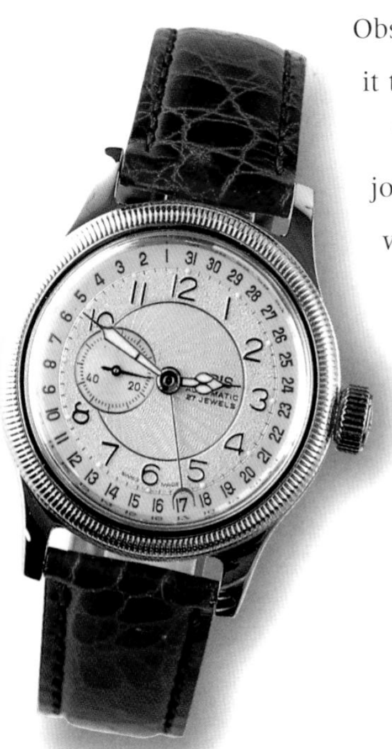

LEFT

BIG CROWN

The luminous hour and minute hands of this distinctive watch are clearly differentiated to avoid confusion at night.

PRODUCT RANGE

Big Crown
Chronometer
Regulator
Pointer
Tonneau
Alarm
Sporty Elegance
Diver's
Rectangular Classic

ORIS

FACT FILE

FOUNDED: 1904
COUNTRY OF ORIGIN: Switzerland
OUTPUT: 100,000 units per annum
MOVEMENT: Mechanical
CEO: Ulrich W. Herzog

Despite losing its own production facilities and most of its customers, the firm had kept its skilled watchmakers and its reputation. Its new Managing Director, Ulrich Herzog, aimed to produce the best watches in the world in their price bracket. He decided to produce only mechanical watches, for which he could use the very best of ETA's movements, "tweaked" by his technicians to give even better performance.

ABOVE
Limited edition mechanical alarm, 1996. A unique and highly collectible mechanical watch.

Today Oris makes only jeweled-lever mechanical watches. Over the years it has introduced many innovations. In 1952 came its first automatic movement with a reserve-power display; in 1968 it obtained full chronometer certification for the Cal 652 movement, and in 1970 it launched its first chronograph. 1988 saw its first mechanical alarm; produced in a limited series, it was based on some A. Schild movements from an earlier epoch which are now collector's items.

In 1989, fifty-one years after its launch, Oris reissued the Pointer Calendar and in 1991 the first Automatic Complication at an affordable price. In 1995 came the Regulateur, another innovation in its field.

Current models include the Oris Mechanical Alarm in a limited edition in 18-karat gold, water-resistant to 100 feet with sapphire crystal and embossed silver dial on a crocodile strap.

Ladies and men's Tonneau models come in stainless-steel cases with PVD-coated surfaces: they are water-resistant, with luminous dials and hands, on strap or bracelet.

A Classic Pointer with a small seconds sub-dial at 9 o'clock has a red pointer hand rotating counterclockwise over a black dial with luminous hands and figures. The case is stainless steel or PVD-plated with a skeleton screwback.

There is also a classic model with a skeleton dial and back for those who really like to look into things. It comes in a stainless-steel water-resistant case with screwback.

BELOW
ORIS BIG CROWN CHRONOMETER

FLAGSHIP LINE

Originally designed for pilots of the U.S. Air Force in World War II, the Big Crown was meant for easy operation when wearing gloves. It became a bestseller even among those who never even thought of flying. In its latest form, it is a precise mechanical chronometer, based on the Valjou 7750 chronograph movement with 1/5th second stop and all the usual functions. Having successfully undergone the regulation 15-day tests, it now carries an Official Chronometer Testing Institute Certificate. It comes in a stainless-steel case with a specially designed matching bracelet with safety buckle.

№36

PATEK PHILIPPE

One of the most prestigious Swiss watch brands of all time had an unlikely beginning in a meeting between a former Polish cavalry officer and an inventive French watchmaker.

In 1832, Antoine de Pradwdzic, fleeing his country after an abortive revolt of the Polish army against Russian Tsar Nicholas I, found himself in Geneva. He took Swiss nationality, changed his name to Patek, and in 1839 joined forces with another expatriate Pole named Czapek, who had some experience in the craft, to make watches. With the help of a small staff, they began producing highly decorative models in the contemporary Geneva fashion at the rate of about 200 a year.

In 1844, when exhibiting at the Paris Exposition, Patek met a young French watchmaker named Adrien Philippe who subsequently joined the firm as technical director, ousting Czapek with whom Patek found himself increasingly at odds. The two young men – Patek was still only 33 – produced a number of innovative models, including the first to have a "free" mainspring and an independent seconds hand. Their aim, they said, was to produce the finest watches in the world.

Their performance matched their ambition – over the next few years they won more than 500 international awards; they received an order from Queen Victoria and entrance to the courts of Europe followed: their clientele included 30 royal personages as well as three popes. In 1851 they registered their company as Patek Philippe & Co. Among the exhibits at Paris had been a tiny watch with a diameter of only 8.46mm, the smallest ever made at that time. In 1868 they modified the design to make a timepiece for Countess Kocewicz; it was the world's first wristwatch, but it took the firm another fifty years to produce a commercially viable version.

Among the inventions produced by the firm were a double chronograph with sweep seconds, a perpetual calendar mechanism, and an improved regulator. All involved much handwork, and in 1865 the total output was not more than 2,500 pieces a year.

ABOVE
GONDOLO
With quartz movement and water-resistant to 82ft, a picture of timeless elegance.

ABOVE
NAUTILUS
Water-resistant to 197ft, with quartz movement and date.

RIGHT
LA FLAMME
Gold watch with quartz movement. A combination of elegance and practicality.

PRODUCT RANGE

Calatrava
Nautilus
Ellipse
Gondolo
Flamme

ABOVE

PATEK PHILIPPE Building in Geneva – headquarters of PP since the firm was founded in 1839.

FACT FILE

FOUNDED: 1839
COUNTRY OF ORIGIN: Switzerland
OUTPUT: 20,000 units per annum
MOVEMENT: Mechanical 75%, quartz 25%
CEO: Philippe Stein

After the death of the two founders toward the end of the 19th century, some of the firm's incentive seemed to die with them, and only in the 1920s did the first wristwatch with perpetual calendar and a man's wrist chronograph watch herald a new burst of creativity. The most famous model from this period was a pocket watch made for the American car magnate Ward Packard. It took six years to make and had 20-odd complications, including a view of the stars as seen from Packard's house in Ohio. (It cost him $16,000 and was recently re-purchased by the company for its museum for $2 million.)

But in spite of its technical expertise the company was short of cash, and in 1932 a new dynasty took over the management. Charles Stern came from a family of craftsmen who had been suppliers to Patek Philippe; his son Henri proved an able businessman who set about improving the company's distribution and expanding its market. When, in 1977, his son Philippe became Managing Director, the brand was re-established worldwide.

Always at the forefront of horological development, Patek Philippe invested in electronics at an early stage. By 1952 it had a battery-operated solid-state clock; ten years later, it developed a master clock system that is still used for timekeeping in Switzerland's airports and public buildings. It was a simple step to integrate this new technology into the company's personal timepieces. Today 80 percent of Patek's ladies' watches and 20 percent of the men's models have slim quartz movements, although men's watches account for three-quarters of the firm's total output.

Patek Philippe's latest complicated wristwatch embodies all the technical skill that has maintained the company's reputation for so long. Model 5035 is a self-winding annual calendar – a watch with a mechanism that recognizes months of 30 and 31 days and needs no adjustment from March 1st to the last day of February the following year, when the date must be advanced mechanically. The self-adjusting date is displayed in an opening at 6 o'clock; the mechanism – which is a world first – is entirely rotary, and

BELOW

New ladies Gondolo. Here, square dials are softened by the harmony of the design.

ABOVE

New ladies Calatrava. Unusual hands and pyramid hour-markers on the dial show what a skilled goldsmith can achieve through angles and polish.

is smoother and more precise. It comes in a water-resistant 18-karat yellow, white, or rose gold or platinum case with sapphire crystal glass and case back. 5039 is a more conventional perpetual calendar with an ultraslim self-winding movement. It has a typical Patek double hobnail case in 18-karat gold and is fitted with an alligator strap. Its restrained pearlescent dial displays month, day, date, and moonphase.

In addition to individual masterpieces, Patek Philippe has a number of collections, most popular of which is the Calatrava line. First established in 1932 it is the classic round wristwatch, epitomized in model 3919, with hobnail bezel, neat Roman numerals, and a porcelain white dial. Its 18-karat gold case is water- resistant to 80 feet, and it has a manually wound mechanical movement.

The latest example of the lady's Calatrava introduced in the 1980s is 4919, which takes the hobnail motif even further by incorporating it in four concentric rings on the bezel. The hour markers echo the motif. It is driven by Patek's own E15 quartz movement. Another new model for ladies is the Gondolo 4866 – a square model with a picture-frame bezel enclosing a simple dial with Roman quarters. It has a quartz movement, a choice of strap or bracelet, and a sapphire crystal on an 18-karat yellow-gold case. Patek Philippe claims to be the only independent watchmaker left in Geneva still making all its own watches.

ABOVE

Automatic perpetual calendar in Patek Philippe's classic hobnail pattern case.

FLAGSHIP LINE

The Calatrava collection, established as the gentleman's classic round wristwatch in 1932, is still the most popular design, in both ladies and men's models. It has a number of variations, comes with handwound, mechanical, or quartz movements, or full complication.

RIGHT

CALATRAVA

PERRELET

It is rare indeed for an entirely new Swiss watch brand to come onto the market. The Perrelet "Dipteros" is just such a brand – completely new, but with an ancient and impressive pedigree. Launched at the 1995 Basel Fair, its unique feature is a double rotor which results in a faster and more balanced winding process.

PRODUCT RANGE

Dipteros I
Dipteros II
Jewelry Collection

PERRELET

Abraham-Louis Perrelet was born into a modest family in Le Locle, Switzerland, in 1729, and by the time he was twenty, he had made up his mind to become a watchmaker. After a short apprenticeship he decided to start out on his own. He was soon designing his own tools to produce watch movements and his workshop became well known for his innovations – he was, for instance, the first in Le Locle to make watches with cylinder escapements. He made all the parts himself and even trained many of Le Locle's subsequently famous watchmakers, among them Frédéric Houriet, known as the "Father of the Swiss chronometer." It is said that Abraham-Louis Breguet himself may have been one of Perrelet's apprentices.

Among the many inventions attributed to Abraham-Louis is the self-winding watch. He overcame several initial problems with the stopping mechanism, and several of his watches have survived to this day, still in good running order. Perrelet was just 40 when he perfected his invention; he spent his whole life in Le Locle and continued to make watches right up to his death in 1826; one of his last creations, which he completed at the age of 96, is housed in the International Museum of Horology at La Chaux de Fonds.

Perrelet's grandson Louis-Frédéric made his home in Paris, where his skills brought him to the attention of the court, and he became watchmaker to Louis XVIII, an honor subsequently confirmed by Charles X and Louis-Philippe. Louis-Frédéric was also an innovator and he is claimed to have invented the split-second chronograph in 1827. When he retired, his son Louis also became a Royal Watchmaker and ran the family business in Paris until 1870.

From such impressive forebears, comes the new company – Perrelet SA – founded in Neuchâtel in 1993

ABOVE
DIPTEROS I
18kt gold self-winding watch with unique double rotor movement, on strap. The 18kt gold upper rotor is in the center mounted on a single large ruby.

ABOVE, RIGHT
DIPTEROS II
Stainless steel mechanical self-winding watch with double rotor. The 18kt upper rotor is on the circumference of the dial.

RIGHT
JEWELRY COLLECTION
A diamond-encrusted example from the jewelry collection.

to market a selection of watches under the Perrelet name. Its Managing Director, Jean-Marie Schaller, bought the rights to the name from a well-known distributor; he was backed by Dr. Flavio Audemars, now the president, whose company had been making watch products for almost a century, and he brought in Jean Perrelet, a direct descendant of Abraham-Louis, as a vice president and member of the board of directors.

ABOVE

Original Abraham-Louis Perrelet watch, from the Beyer Museum. The watchmaking origins of the Perrelet family go back to the early years of the 18th century.

The firm's charter commits it to respect the traditions of the founding father and to make only Swiss self-winding timepieces of the highest quality. The firm's first production was the Perrelet Dipteros collection of automatic watches for men and women.

The Dipteros (Greek for two-winged) has a double rotor, which is designed to give a more constant supply of energy leading to improved running stability. The two rotors revolve around a common shaft and are linked by wheels which mesh with a specially supported pinion. The lower rotor corresponds to the oscillating weight of a conventional self-winding system; the upper one, which is mounted on a gigantic watch jewel, is situated on the dial side of the movement and can be seen through the crystal.

Two from Perrelet's jewelry collection. Every Perrelet watch incorporates one or more valid and innovative elements of design.

FACT FILE

FOUNDED: 1993
COUNTRY OF ORIGIN: Switzerland
OUTPUT: 2,500 pieces per annum
MOVEMENT: Self-winding mechanical
CEO: Jean-Marie Schaller

The Dipteros I men's models use a DH95 caliber based on an ETA 2892-2 mechanical movement with 24 jewels; the ladies' version has 28 jewels and is fitted with a Cal DD95 on an ETA 2671 movement. The cases are stainless steel, steel and 18-karat gold, or all gold; they have a pressure caseback, are water-resistant to 100 feet, and are fitted with a sapphire crystal and an ostrich leather strap or metal bracelet.

There are 72 models in the current Perrelet line, which now includes Dipteros II with an exterior upper rotor a limited edition in pink gold – the 555 – and a jewelry collection with gem-set bezels on 18-karat gold cases in men's and ladies' sizes on alligator straps or 18-karat gold bracelets.

FLAGSHIP LINE

Dipteros I with central upper rotor and Dipteros II with exterior upper rotor are the two flagship models.

RIGHT

DIPTEROS I

Nº38

PIAGET

Many Swiss watchmaking companies go back a long way, but it is rare to find one that is still in the hands of a member of the original family. Although Piaget became a part of the Richemont Group in 1988, the day-to-day control remained in the hands of Yves Piaget, great-grandson of the founder.

ABOVE
MINI DANCER
Smaller version of Dancer, with 18kt gold case and bracelet and gold dial.

Georges Piaget is given the credit for founding the company in 1874 in the village of La Côte aux Fées. In the early days, the workshop would have been in the upper part of the farmhouse itself, but in 1890 Georges was able to rent the ground floor of a chapel. Piaget specialized in lever escapements, and the quality of his work soon established him with some of Switzerland's most famous names; account books of the period show Breguet, Audemars Piguet, Vacheron Constantin, and Zenith among his clients.

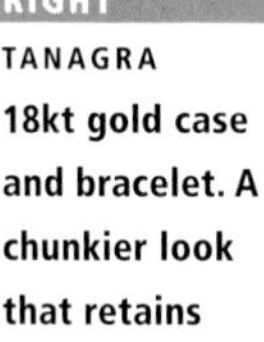

RIGHT
TANAGRA
18kt gold case and bracelet. A chunkier look that retains all the elegance of other lines.

Part of Piaget's work was in finishing partially mounted movements for other manufacturers and Timothée Piaget, who had taken over from his father in 1911, decided to assemble and sell complete watches, although the firm still did not sign them. His son, Gérald, succeeded him in the mid-1940s, and decided that the firm needed its own workshop, which he proceeded to build in La Côte aux Fées in 1945. Piaget was now an established "timepiece factory" and controlled the whole manufacturing chain, from making rough movements to assembling complete and sophisticated watches. The name Piaget first appeared on the dials at this time. With the purchase of two workshops in Geneva which made straps, cases, and dials, Piaget became a true *manufacture*. Piaget's fourth chairman was Valentin, Gérald's brother. A technical man, he laid down the policy for the future: to develop the thinnest watch movements in the world. The launch of Piaget's ultrathin watch was a turning point in

PRODUCT RANGE

Gouverneur
Georges Piaget
Piaget Polo
Emperador
Possession
Citea

LEFT
POLO
Simple and elegant, with champagne dial, 18kt gold case and bracelet.

ABOVE
Gouverneur in yellow gold, with hand-engraved gold dial and applied gold indexes.

the company's history. Valentin was also the first to introduce a quartz movement into Haute Joaillerie watches, for by now Piaget was in the echelons of the elite. The aim at Piaget was to opt for quality rather than quantity and to produce only a limited number of pieces.

By the end of the 1980s, Yves Piaget, who had taken over, saw that a change of direction was essential. The decision to join the Richemont Group was not easy for the inheritor of such a private company. However, it has given the company the backing of a group specializing in luxury products which already included Cartier, Baume et Mercier, and Yves St. Laurent, while allowing him to keep Piaget's separate identity.

Since the 1960s Piaget has been renowned for its Haute Joaillerie watches and its ultrathin movements allowed it to pioneer the use of hard stones such as lapis lazuli, coral, mother-of-pearl, and tiger eye in an unusual and exciting variety of dials. Contemporary collections include the Georges Piaget watch, a tribute to the founder, with a manually wound hand-built movement. The 120th anniversary commemorative watches in a limited series of just 120 pieces each in platinum, yellow, rose and white gold have a specially created mechanical movement only 2.9mm thick with a 38-hour power reserve. There is a Piaget Polo line of elegant sporty watches, and the exclusively mechanical Gouverneur with an automatic certified chronometer movement with a 50-hour power reserve comes in a pink-gold case limited to 200 pieces with sapphire crystal front and back, or in yellow-gold with moonphase. There is a Rectangle or l'Ancienne in white gold with a mechanical handwound movement, and a cushion-shaped model called Emperador in yellow gold with a self-winding movement. The Citea has a round case and a dial with a flange, and is available in both ladies' and men's sizes in yellow gold; the lady's model has a quartz movement and is on a bracelet; the man's has an automatic movement with a 45-hour power reserve and comes on a strap. Exclusively for ladies is the quartz Possession with models in yellow gold.

FACT FILE

FOUNDED: 1874
COUNTRY OF ORIGIN: Switzerland
OUTPUT: Information not available
MOVEMENT: Mechanical, quartz
CEO: Yves Piaget

BELOW
CITEA

FLAGSHIP LINE

Piaget says it has no flagship line, since many of the watches are very limited editions, but the Citea model is probably the nearest thing to a "popular" line.

Rado

In 1917, in the closing stages of World War I, the brothers Fitz, Ernst, and Werner Schlup started production of watch movements in their parents' house in Lengnau. They sold their products to American importers, a connection that lasted for the next thirty years. By the end of World War II, Schlup and Co. had built up a thriving business in watch movements, helped by post-war shortages in the United States. Competition was just around the corner, however, and the company started making complete watches for other firms.

ABOVE
LA COUPOLE CERAMIQUE
"Jubilé" model, in midnight blue, with sapphire crystal glass.

In 1947 Dr. Paul Lüthi, whose wife was a member of the family, joined the company. More an academic than a businessman, he was nevertheless to shape the firm's destiny for the next 40 years. He saw that the production of private-label watches had a limited future and set about building up the firm's own brand, which at that time was Exacto. With much competition on his doorstep, the pioneering Dr. Lüthi set off for Argentina and Brazil, where he achieved considerable success. His efforts to expand further were thwarted by objections to the name as being too descriptive, so he coined a new one – Rado – and set off once more – this time to the Far East. Over the years this enterprising man built up considerable connections, to the extent that 70 percent of the firm's output was going to Asia Pacific. He called the most popular design "Starliner"; it was a robust product, with a water-resistance of 12 atmospheres, thanks to a system exclusive to Rado.

Many of the watches the company sold to Hong Kong had gold cases which frequently got scratched and needed repolishing. Lüthi and the firm's designer Lederrey set out to find a scratchproof material. They experimented for some time with tungsten and titanium carbide before finding the right compound; they produced their first case in 1962 and called the watch the DiaStar. It was a sensation both in design and construction, and with it, Lüthi was finally able to crack the Swiss market.

RIGHT
DIASTAR CERAMICA
Bracelet, case and crown in scratchproof high-tech ceramics, with four diamonds on the dial.

ABOVE
DIA QUEEN
In high-tech ceramic, very light and comfortable to wear, and scratch-resistant.

PRODUCT RANGE

DiaStar Anatom
DiaStar Ceramica
DiaStar Integral
DiaStar Sintra
La Coupole
La Coupole Céramique
DiaQueen

RADO

ABOVE

Sleek, comfortable and beautiful. Rado DiaQueen is set off still further by the addition of diamonds on the bracelet and framing the dial.

In 1968 Rado, like others, sought protection from the winds of change by joining the General Watch Co., a subsidiary of ASUAG which later merged with SSIH to form SMH, the giant conglomerate already mentioned.

As a result, Rado had the backing of resources far beyond a small family business. From the launch of DiaStar (Dia = hard as a diamond; Star = as brilliant as a star in the sky), Rado established an irrefutable international reputation for scratchproof watches and innovative designs.

The oval original was followed by a round case; in 1969 came a rectangular one – the DiaStar 10 – and in 1972 the first gold-colored oval; DiaStar 13 was the most successful model in Rado's history. 1974 saw the first quartz DiaStar and in 1987 came La Coupole, a round watch with a domed sapphire crystal which protected the whole watch surface from rim to rim. The next breakthrough was in 1989 with the Ceramic, in which the bracelet as well as the case and crown were made form high-tech materials; this breakthrough was followed by La Coupole Ceramique, with a simple bracelet also formed from ceramic elements.

Other Rado models from the 1980s and '90s are the Manhattan, a super water-resistant (24ATM) rectangular model; the Florence, a lady's model of revolutionary design; the Captain Cook, a diver's model for men and women; and the DiaStar Integral, Rado's first model with a bracelet made from high-tech ceramic elements.

FACT FILE

FOUNDED: 1917
COUNTRY OF ORIGIN: Switzerland
OUTPUT: Information not available
MOVEMENT: Mechanical and quartz
CEO: Roland Streule

Rado's latest innovation is the Anatom Multi, a square-cased model on a bracelet, with seven functions – digital time, running seconds and date, day and date, timer, second time zone, chronograph, and alarm – all on command at a turn of the crown. Dr. Lüthi, who is still Chairman of the Board, is proud of Rado's latest creation,which he says follows the firm's philosophy that he has upheld for so long – a pioneering spirit and continuity in style.

BELOW

ANATOM MULTI

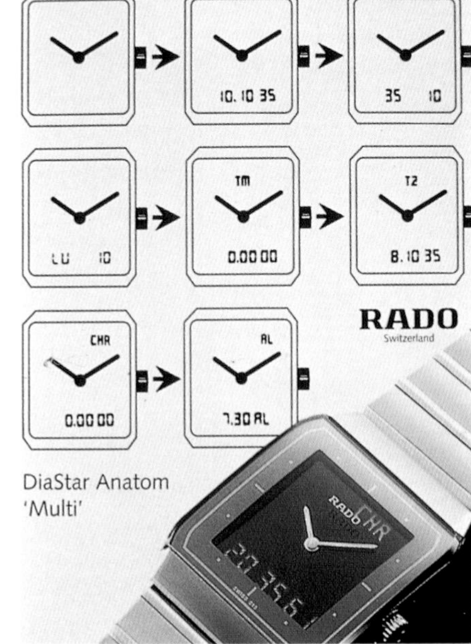

FLAGSHIP LINE

The most popular lines are the DiaStar Anatom and the DiaStar Integral.

№40

Raymond Weil

Raymond Weil is one of the few brands of watches bearing the name of the man who actually makes them (individual creative horologists apart).

The company was founded in 1976 by Raymond Weil and Simone Bédat. Raymond Weil, a Genevan, had worked for a Geneva watch firm for 30 years, rising to be the head of the company. Then, at the height of the crisis in the Swiss watchmaking industry, he decided to found his own company. Simone Bédat had worked with Raymond Weil in the sales department of the Geneva firm since 1959. She took over the design of the new company's watches – a responsibility which she has shared with her son Christian since 1990.

The fourth member of the management team is Olivier Bernheim, in charge of the company's financial and external affairs. Married to one of Raymond Weil's daughters, he also shares responsibility for marketing and sales with Christian Bédat.

In the twenty years since its inception, Raymond Weil has become a major producer among Switzerland's watch houses. With global sales of around 600,000 pieces a year, it claims to rank fourth in the hierarchy.

There are eight collections in Raymond Weil's total output, many of them named after pieces of classical or operatic music. The main sub-brand is Parsifal, accounting for 35 percent of sales worldwide, followed by Fidelio, Tango, and Toccata. The models are mostly quartz, with about 10 percent ETA mechanical movements used in special watches, and are divided fairly evenly between men's and ladies' watches. Parsifal, launched in 1991, has a distinctive bezel with embossed studs, a shield to protect the crown, and a screwdown back. It is available in 18-karat gold, stainless steel and 18-karat gold, and its 18-karat gold-with-diamonds model marked the brand's entry into the luxury watch sector.

There are approximately 50 different designs in the Parsifal line – round case, square case, a sports version in an 18-karat gold case, and an integral bracelet model. Most have quartz

PRODUCT RANGE

Parsifal
Fidelio
Tango
Toccata

ABOVE
GENTS MODEL
9833
18kt yellow gold plated case on strap with Swiss quartz movement.

BELOW
Golden Eagle, with striking octagonal face.

LEFT
LADIES MODEL
5857
18kt white gold plated case on matching integral bracelet. Swiss quartz movement.

ABOVE
Integrated Parsifal comes in a square steel case with 18kt gold bezel. The curved, tapered bracelet blends perfectly with the case.

movements; all are water-resistant to at least 100 feet and have scratch-resistant crystals. The Parsifal Evolution, launched in 1996, is an elegant gold-cased model on bracelet with pink *clous de Paris* dial. It is available in two sizes.

Another recent innovation is the Parsifal Chronograph in a stainless-steel case with satin-finished steel bezel and tachymeter. It has the customary sub-dials for hours, minutes, and seconds, a date window at 3 o'clock, and an ETA mechanical chronograph movement. It is water-resistant to 165 feet and comes on a specially developed black high-resistance fabric strap.

BELOW
Traviata. Many collections are named after pieces of classical and operatic music.

Another new model with a mechanical movement is the Parsifal Sport Automatic in a stainless-steel case, water-resistant to 165 feet, on a matching steel bracelet with a protected screwdown crown.

Fidelio dates from 1985 and has a more traditional appearance, with slender cases mostly with 18-karat gold-plated bracelets. It comes in two sizes, with a choice of round or square case and a variety of dials.

Tango, launched ten years after Fidelio, is an elegant 18-karat gold-plated sports watch with a round case in steel, steel and 18-karat gold plate, or all 18-karat gold plate. It has a quartz movement and is water-resistant to 165 feet. There is a diver's version with rotating bezel which is water-resistant to 330 feet.

BELOW
PARSIFAL

One of Raymond Weil's first models was called the Golden Eagle, with a distinctive octagonal case in stainless steel and golden studs on the bezel, matched by smaller studs on an integrated flat-link bracelet.

Another of Raymond Weil's earlier successes was Traviata, a gold integrated bracelet watches for men and women with unusual dials like stained-glass windows.

FACT FILE

FOUNDED: 1976
COUNTRY OF ORIGIN: Switzerland
OUTPUT: 600,000 pieces per annum
MOVEMENT: Quartz 90%, mechanical 10%
CEO: Raymond Weil

FLAGSHIP LINE

Raymond Weil's flagship line is the Parsifal Collection with its variety of cases, dials, executions (both quartz and mechanical) and finishes.

Rolex

The story of Rolex begins at the turn of the century. After a few years on the clerical side of the watchmaking industry in Switzerland, Hans Wilsdorf, at the age of 24, set up his own company in England.

PRODUCT RANGE

Oyster
Oyster Perpetual
Datejust
Air king
Explorer
Submariner
Sea Dweller
Yachtmaster
Cosmograph
GMT Master
Cellini
Tudor

By 1910 the quality of Wilsdorf's watches was such that one of them obtained the first official chronometer certificate ever awarded to a wristwatch, followed four years later by a Class A Certificate, the highest award from Kew Observatory – again, the first such award ever given to a wristwatch.

Wilsdorf was determined to produce watches just as accurate in quantity for sale to a wider public. Soon after the end of World War I, he moved his headquarters from England to Geneva and renamed his firm the Montres Rolex SA. (He had already registered the name Rolex in 1908.)

Wilsdorf then set his technicians the task of designing a really waterproof case. By 1926 he had a prototype; its bezel and back were screwed onto the central carcass using a lead seal, the crown was similarly screwed onto the case: the only potentially weak point – the glass – was tackled by accurately machining an artificial crystal and sealing it to the bezel. Samples were tested under water for three weeks; they showed no sign of moisture penetration and no variation of performance. The Rolex Oyster had arrived.

Wilsdorf was a born publicist. He persuaded a London typist to wear a Rolex Oyster during an attempt to swim the English Channel. When Mercedes Gleitz stepped ashore at Dover, photographers were there to see that the watch was still working perfectly.

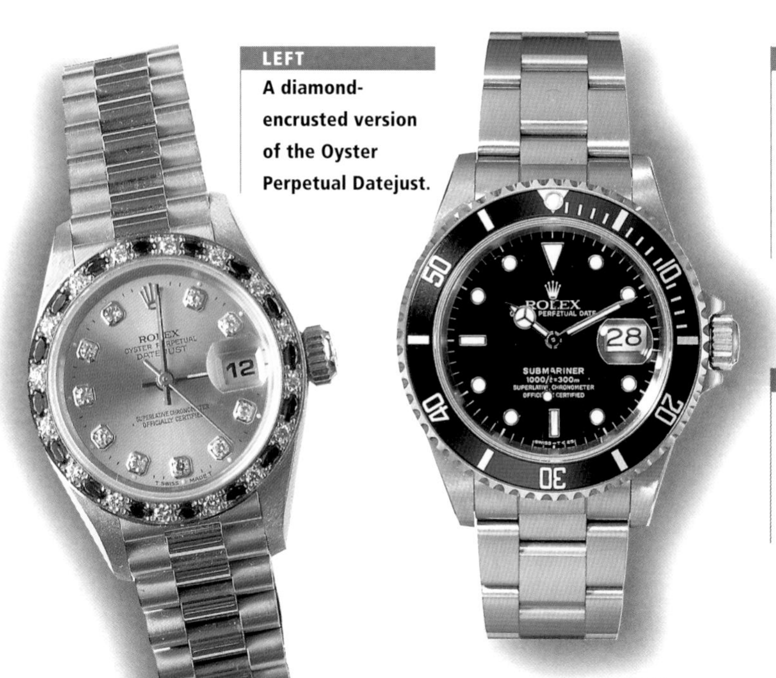

LEFT
A diamond-encrusted version of the Oyster Perpetual Datejust.

LEFT
SUBMARINER
The first wristwatch to have a guaranteed water-resistance of 330ft.

RIGHT
YACHTMASTER
This handsome watch has a distinctly nautical appearance.

But Wilsdorf was still not satisfied. His watches were waterprooof, but they still had to be wound by hand and that meant unscrewing the crown. A number of firms were already producing self-winding wristwatches based on Harwood's invention, which depended On an oscillating weight consisting of a circular disk pivoted at its center and rotating through 130 degrees with a stop at each end.

Wilsdorf set out to find a better solution. In 1931 he introduced an entirely new principle, which utilized a rotor with a 360-degree oscillation. It was subsequently complemented by a slipping clutch device, and together they comprised the Rolex Perpetual system of automatic winding which, when its patent ran out in 1945, was to be copied by almost every maker of self-winding wristwatches.

FACT FILE

FOUNDED: 1905
COUNTRY OF ORIGIN: Switzerland
OUTPUT: 1 million units per annum
MOVEMENT: Mechanical and quartz
CEO: Andre Heineger

Early Rolex Oyster models had a cushion-shaped case. In the 1940s a round case appeared, and from then on, the basic design with its distinctive milled edge became the international image of the Rolex Oyster. Each Oyster case is carved from a single block of platinum, 18-karat gold, or stainless steel. It takes over 100 processes to turn it into a finished case, and a further 35 operations to fashion the famous Oyster Crown. The Oyster has remained more or less the same for 50 years.

The "Datejust," launched in 1945, was the first chronometer with automatic date change; in the 1950s Rolex introduced the Submariner, the first wristwatch to have a guaranteed water-resistance of 330 feet. In 1971 Rolex launched the Sea Dweller for divers; fitted with a helium valve to cope with decompression, it was guaranteed to a depth of 2,000 feet. The famous Oyster crown was subsequently adapted to incorporate a Triplock system which made descent to 4,000 feet possible.

LEFT
All Rolex Chronometers bear the inscription "superlative Chronometer Officially Certified."

Not all Rolex's achievements were underwater. Edmund Hillary took a Rolex Explorer to Everest's 29,028-foot summit in 1953, and on an archaeological dig in Afghanistan, Rolex was found to be the only watch which could keep out the all-pervading sand.

ABOVE
The Rolex worldwide headquarters situated in Geneva, Switzerland.

In 1963 Wilsdorf was succeeded by André Heiniger, who was responsible for taking Rolex to its present international eminence. The company was soon compelled to seek larger premises, moving to a new modern building just outside the city.

LEFT
The original Rolex oyster in its "cushion" case, created in 1926.

Rolex has one of the most comprehensive lines of watches in the upper echelons of the Swiss watch industry. Under the banner of the Rolex Oyster Collection, it offers, in men's models (which are in the majority) simple self-winding watches in steel cases; automatic chronometers (Rolex produces roughly half of all the chronometers certified by COSC) with date, day date, or dual time zone displays, right up to diamond-set models in platinum. All have the famous Oyster doubly protected screwdown crown and are water-resistant to 330 feet. They all have sapphire crystals and, except for the Oyster Quartz, have self-winding mechanical movements.

For the ladies there are Oyster Perpetual models in steel or 18-karat gold, many also with certified chronometer movements, and a selection of diamond-set jewelry watches.

All Rolex watches are available on the company's own collection of bracelets, which come in a number of sizes and finishes, tailored to suit particular models.

OTHER COLLECTIONS

Rolex created the Cellini collection in homage to the 16th-century sculptor and goldsmith, Benvenuto Cellini. It exists only in 18-karat gold on a strap or gold bracelets, many integrated with the finely wrought cases which come in a variety of attractive designs. Here, too, are diamond-set models for both men and women; there is a small quartz collection, but the majority have handwound mechanical movements.

Rolex also markets the Tudor line with quartz or mechanical movements; these models have the Oyster crown, water-resistance to 165 feet, and come in two sizes of case in steel or yellow metal at prices geared to the less expensive sector of the market.

RIGHT
OYSTER PERPETUAL DATEJUST

FLAGSHIP LINE

The Oyster Perpetual Datejust is the flagship collection in Rolex's comprehensive line. A self-winding certified chronometer in steel or 18-karat gold water-resistant to 330 feet, it is available on a variety of bracelets, the most popular being the President.

№42

Daniel Roth

Daniel Roth's interest in horology was born when, at the age of 6, he moved with his family to Nice where his grandfather ran a watch business. At the age of 14, he was enrolled as a student at the Nice School for Watchmaking; his professor enlightened him to the fact that the most beautiful watches in the world came from the Valleé de Joux in Switzerland, northeast of Geneva. When he was 18, Daniel Roth made his way there.

ABOVE

Automatic Chronograph. The elegance of the superb finish is enhanced by the distinctive dials.

His first job was with Jaeger-LeCoultre in Le Sentier. Soon he moved to Audemars Piguet, in the neighboring village of Le Brassus, where he spent four years specializing in the construction of some of the smallest and thinnest watch movements in the world. Soon he had earned a reputation for his work on ultrathin watches which reached the ears of the Chaumet Brothers in Paris, who were at that time interested in reviving the name of the greatest watchmaker of all time, Abraham-Louis Breguet.

They offered him the task. He accepted and spent another year at the advanced "Ecole d'Horlogie" in Le Sentier specializing in the construction of very complicated mechanical movements. Daniel Roth devoted himself to reviving Breguet's art; in particular, he adapted Breguet's pocket watch designs to wristwatch form. Within 13 years, the name Breguet was once again one to be reckoned with in the world of *haute horlogerie*. It was inevitable that this young horologist should want to branch out on his own.

PRODUCT RANGE

Daniel Roth does not name any lines as such, only individual pieces.

DANIEL ROTH

In 1988, still only 43, Daniel Roth set up his own workshop in Le Sentier, close to the lake, to create his own individual masterpieces that combined traditional haute horlogerie with a creative touch. There are now 15 employees – young but experienced craftsmen – who work with him to produce a limited number of watches, inspired by the four principles he has laid down. They are Creativity – the Daniel Roth watch has a distinctive profile; Integrity – watches crafted meticulously to give precise timekeeping; Exclusivity – limited and numbered editions, some as few as 30 pieces; Perfection – an aim as difficult to define as to achieve. All Daniel Roth will say is that perfection is what he and his team strive for – it is what turns a good watch into a masterpiece.

LEFT

Glittering stars – Lady Diamonds and Lady Diamonds and Rubies.

FACT FILE

FOUNDED: 1988
COUNTRY OF ORIGIN: Switzerland
OUTPUT: Information not available
MOVEMENT: Mechanical 90%
CEO: Daniel Roth

RIGHT
Minute Repeater with perpetual calendar, a fine example of the creativity integral to every Daniel Roth watch.

Except for complications, Daniel Roth does not make his own movements. He chooses the most suitable from those by Piguet, Jaeger-LeCoultre, Lemania, Girard Perregaux, and Zenith. His collection includes stainless-steel sports bracelet models which won the Watch of the Year award in 1995 and Best Bracelet of the Year in 1996, and are available in 1996 on a strap, in a GMT or automatic version, and with an 18-karat gold case if preferred.

But it is in the field of complicated watches that Daniel Roth's international reputation lies. His Tourbillon with a double face has a hand-built handwound mechanical movement in a typical Daniel Roth case in 18-karat yellow, pink, or white gold or PT950 platinum. It has a sapphire crystal and a unique date and power-reserve indicator on the case back.

His automatic chronograph comes only in stainless steel, with three versions of dial, silver, pink, or anthracite. The movement is a fast beat 36,000 vph, with 42 jewels, has 1/10th second flyback hand, and subsidiary dials for hours, minutes and seconds. It has a date window at 5 o'clock. The movement is finished by hand with Côtes de Genève decoration, visible through the sapphire crystal back. It has a power reserve of 50 hours.

Other recent Roth masterpieces included a pair of ladies jeweled models, the familiar case set with a choice of diamonds or rubies on matching bracelets. Complications included a Single Face Tourbillon and a minute repeater with perpetual calendar.

ABOVE
Daniel Roth's Masterpiece, the Automatic Chronograph, is accurate to 1/10 of a second. Shown here in steel.

FLAGSHIP LINE

The stainless-steel sports watches, introduced in 1996 at a starting price of less than half of any previous Daniel Roth watch, are highly acclaimed. The Tourbillon model is also particularly successful.

RIGHT
Style, elegance, originality and grace. All are incorporated in Daniel Roth's outstanding Single Face Tourbillon.

SEIKO

It is tempting to regard Seiko, one of Japan's leading watch and clock manufacturers, as a phenomenon of the hi-tech revolution, but in fact it has a pedigree as long as many of its Swiss contemporaries.

A Tokyo jeweler named Kitaro Hattori formed K. Hattori and Co. in 1881 and next year a second company, Seikosha was formed to meet a growing demand for clocks which followed Japan's adoption of the 24-hour time zone. In 1895 Hattori started to produce pocket watches, and in 1918 wristwatches.

Hattori launched his first wristwatch in 1923 under the name Seiko. By 1936 Seiko was responsible for 60 percent of Japan's horological output.

ABOVE
DIVER'S KINETIC
Diver's 200m Kinetic – water-resistant to 328ft.

ABOVE
KINETIC SLIM
The advantages of Kinetic technology combined with a slim elegance.

After World War II, Seiko resumed watch production, producing over half of Japan's total output of 2.5m pieces in 1953, and ten years later its reputation was given a boost by the firm's appointment as official timekeeper to the Tokyo Olympic Games. Seiko not only provided stopwatches for the officials, but unveiled its latest invention, a portable quartz chronometer. It was inevitable that such a device would be developed for personal timekeeping.

BELOW
KINETIC SQ 100
Titanium and gold plated case and bracelet. Offers quartz accuracy without battery.

In 1969 Seiko launched the Astron, the world's first commercially viable, mass-produced quartz wristwatch. Such a revolutionary concept was matched by equally innovative production techniques and marketing tactics. Seiko's export markets, lost to the company during and after the war, were vigorously courted. Initially the firm concentrated on the analog mode – with conventional dial and hands – for which they perceived a consumer preference, although they later introduced the world's first LCD watch with digital display.

In the 1980s, to broaden its base of operations, and to widen its appeal to different sectors of the market, two other brands were introduced under the Hattori banner – Pulsar and Lorus – and the Swiss firm of Jean Lassale was acquired to gain a foothold in the luxury watch market.

Meanwhile the company continued to develop its high-tech resources. In 1982 it launched a TV watch, and in 1984 the first computer wristwatch. The Intelligent Quartz line followed,

PRODUCT RANGE

Kinetic
Kinetic Slim
Macchina Sportiva
The Great Blue
Rivoli
Classic
Titanium Collection

SEIKO

which included a chronograph with 1/10th second timer, alarm, and automatic calendar, a world time alarm which could be set for any time zone and also had a chronograph movement with calendar, and the "Scubamaster," which could store data on up to 30 dives.

But Seiko's real breakthrough came with the introduction of the Kinetic AGS (Automatic Generating System) wristwatch in 1994. The rotation of an oscillating weight, as in an automatic mechanical watch, activated by the wearer's movements, generates electricity, which is then stored in a capacitor and released as needed to drive the quartz movement. The "quartz watch without a battery" won an award for the Best New Product of 1994.

FACT FILE

FOUNDED: 1881
COUNTRY OF ORIGIN: Japan
OUTPUT: Information not available
MOVEMENT: Quartz 90%, mechanical 10%
CEO: Hasahiro Sakimoto

Increasingly sophisticated technology resulted in smaller calibers, making ladies' models and slim dress watches practical, as well as allowing the introduction of a power-reserve indicator. A further innovation was a form of luminescence called Lumibrite, for hands and hour markers.

ABOVE **This pair of ladies bracelet watches demonstrates the elegance and variety of Seiko's lines.**

Among the company's latest models are the Macchina Sportiva, created for Seiko by the Italian designer Giorgetto Guigiaro, a line of six chronographs and two combination quartz watch timers.

The modern case in stainless steel is water-resistant to 20ATM, has a sapphire crystal, and comes on bracelet or "swim-safe" leather strap. The movement is a 1/5th-second chronograph with split timer, the usual elapsed-time indicators, and an alarm. An unusual feature are the brick orange and sky blue dials. The hands and hour markers are Lumibrite.

Another line is the Seiko Great Blue, a sports watch collection with a theme color of blue. Available in calendar or chronograph versions in an elegant tonneau-shaped case on bracelet or swimproof blue strap, it comes in two sizes, both with Lumibrite hands and hour markers.

Exclusive to women is the Rivoli collection, a stunning original design in a symmetrical case, on an integral bracelet; while for men there is a classic square stainless-steel alarm chronograph on a bracelet with a distinguished pink-gold dial.

FLAGSHIP LINE

Seiko's flagship is the Kinetic line of battery-operated quartz models that run on electricity generated by the wearer's own movements. The collection includes ladies and gents models, slim dress watches, and chronographs.

RIGHT **KINETIC**

Nº44

Alain Silberstein

More than most, perhaps, the watches of Alain Silberstein are immediately recognizable by their unique case design and highly individual brightly colored dials. But these are no "pop" watches; they are serious contributions to art in timekeeping, with top-quality movements, precious metal cases, and superbly finished straps and bracelets. Frenchman Alain Silberstein is primarily a designer. Having studied industrial design at the School of Applied Arts in Paris, he worked in interior design for 15 years; meanwhile, he collected watches.

PRODUCT RANGE

Krono
Marine
Bodoni
Mikro

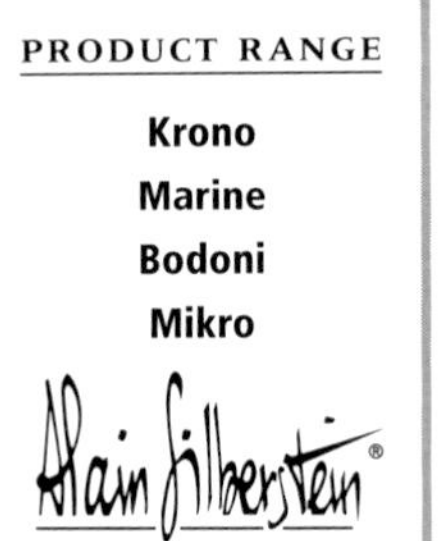

His first creation was a chronograph. He couldn't find one on the market that he liked well enough to wear, so he designed his own. It was based on the ETA 7750 movement, and around it he built a decidedly original case. He took it to the Basel Fair in 1987, along with a couple of quartz models, and in spite of being stuck up on the third floor, immediately found himself taking orders, notably from Italy and Japan – his Japanese contact then is to this day his distributor in Japan.

In 1989, with his wife who is also a designer, he opened Alain Silberstein Creations Ltd., his own watch company. He insists that he is a designer, not a watchmaker, and depends on reliable supplies and four in-house watchmakers to attend to the technicalities.

He moved to Besançon, center of the French watchmaking industry, although much of the help this young Frenchman received was from the Swiss. He is particularly appreciative of the support he has received from ETA, who provided much detailed information and training which helped him acquire the basic knowledge – and not least the terminology – to enable him to write the specifications of his models.

BELOW

PERPETUAL CALENDAR MODEL

In platinum on strap. Automatic mechanical movement with certified chronometer certificate. The calendar aperture is on the back of the watch.

RIGHT

MARINE GMT

Stainless steel with leather strap, two time zones and automatic movement.

RIGHT

BAUHAUS KRONO

With stopwatch. All Alan Silberstein watches come in a case with additional bracelet.

Now he has his own premises, employs about ten people, and plans to produce about 3,000 watches a year – about 90 percent of them for men – aimed he says at the 25–40 age group. He uses ETA, Piaget, and Breguet movements.

He concentrates his cases in three shapes – the circle, the square, and the triangle – and favors three strong colors – yellow, red, and blue. If he has a role model, it is the Bauhaus, based on the designs of that design movement of the 1920s.

As well as watches, Alain Silberstein designs unique and equally colourful clocks using traditional French movements.

FACT FILE

FOUNDED: 1989
COUNTRY OF ORIGIN: France
OUTPUT: 3,000 pieces per annum
MOVEMENT: Mechanical
CEO: Alain Silberstein

ABOVE
Krono. The unmistakable bold and exciting design of an Alain Silberstein watch.

Silberstein's watches are truly collector's pieces. The Krono Classic is an automatic chronograph watch based on the Valjou 7751 with day, date, and month, and a full Chronometer Certificate. Limited to 500 numbered pieces, it has a stainless-steel case water-resistant to 330 feet and a sapphire crystal front and back.

The Marine is a super sports version of the Krono. It is an automatic chronograph with power reserve and date. Its stainless steel case is water resistant to 660 feet, has a uni-directional turning bezel, and prominent luminous hour markers. Its certified chronometer movement can be seen through the sapphire case back. Other versions of the Marine have dual time zones and split seconds hands. All are fitted with stainless-steel bracelets and are produced in limited numbered editions.

LEFT
A riot of color – Marine Chronograph.

Other models include the Bodoni, a tribute to a famous Italian typographical designer whose numerals are used on the dial, and the Mikro, a small lady's automatic with sweep seconds hand and calendar.

Top of the line is the Tourbillon Night and Day, which consists of two "poetic" watches created in 1994 in platinum to symbolize passing time. One watch represents Day; the other, with a black dial, Night. The tourbillons are visible through windows in the dials which carry stylized sun, moon, and stars.

FLAGSHIP LINE

Alain Silberstein says he has no flagship line but takes his inspiration from the Bauhaus movement of the 1920s founded by German architect Walter Gropius.

№45

Swatch

The story of Swatch really begins in 1978, when Switzerland's watch industry was under great pressure from Japan. The inexpensive watch market, which Swiss pin-lever watches had previously dominated, had been virtually lost to the new quartz models from the Far East.

PRODUCT RANGE

There are literally hundreds of names. The collection falls into the following major groups:

Original Swatch
Straight Swatch
Pop Swatch
Swatch Aqua Chrono
Swatch Solar
Swatch Irony

swatch

Dr. Ernst Thomke, then head of ETA, the movement division of SMH, challenged his technicians to beat the Japanese – he wanted a better, slimmer quartz movement. He called the project "Delirium Tremens" because he thought he was crazy to attempt it!

Six months later, ETA produced a prototype movement. It was 2mm high and was the thinnest quartz movement in the world. One of its features was that it made use of the caseback as the backplate; it was launched as the Concord Delirium. The techniques gained from its production were later adopted to produce an answer to the competition.

RIGHT

CHRONOGRAPH

Plastic case, leather strap, with quartz chronograph movement.

A quartz watch produced semi-automatically, its components were reduced from 91 to just 51 parts, in a plastic waterproof case, shock-resistant, durable, and most important, affordable. It was March, 1983, and they called it the Swatch.

Barely a year passed before the millionth Swatch rolled off the production line. By 1985 production had reached 10 million; Pop Swatch and Maxi Swatch were introduced, and in 1987 the first-ever Christmas Special was released – it was the beginning of an annual event, for by now collectors were becoming interested in Swatch. 1989 saw the first Swatch Telecom product – the Twinphone. By now well over 50 million Swatches had been sold, and the "Puff" Specials in a pristine set of six sold for a mind-boggling £80,000 ($120,000)!

BELOW

BIG SEVEN

Plastic case and bracelet, quartz movement, water-resistant to 100ft.

In 1990 two new Swatch models, the Chronograph and the Scuba, were launched and the following year saw the first mechanical Swatch. In 1992 the first-ever Swatch automatic was introduced. The Swatch Collectors' Club was formed; within a year it had 75,000 members worldwide. Also introduced was the Swatch Pager – the first analog wristwatch with an integrated radio receiver.

LEFT

Kishoo. Around 150 different designs are introduced each year.

FACT FILE

FOUNDED: 1983
COUNTRY OF ORIGIN: Switzerland
OUTPUT: 20 million per annum
MOVEMENT: Mechanical, quartz
CEO: Nicholas Hayek

By 1993, a decade after its launch, Swatch had reached annual sales of 20 million units and was the SMH Group's core product. Its low prices may not have produced large profits, but the huge cash flow helped to cover the cost of developing and producing the rest of the Group's productions, to say nothing of the help it gave to the manufacturing processes of some of its more expensive stable companions.

That year also saw a collaboration with London designer Vivienne Westwood to produce "The Orb" Pop Swatch, and the British allocation of 1,000 pieces sold out in four hours.

By 1994 over 130 million Swatches had been sold, and the AquaChrono, with traditional chronograph functions, a scuba bezel, and water resistance to 660 feet, was launched.

Around 150 different designs are introduced each year in four seasonal collections. Swatch Collectors' Club members, now well over 100,000, are kept informed of trends by magazine and have access to special Swatch designs not available to the general public.

The current Swatch collection has a baffling multiplicity of names. "Themes of the Times," is the signature tune, with Ethnosense, Nat Code, Invisibles, Baby Faces, Artists, and "Tech is Cool." What they mean is anybody's guess, but no doubt fans and collectors know the difference.

The most notable departure from the early image of pretty plastic is the introduction of Swatch Irony – a new collection of twelve models in stainless-steel cases. Keeping up with the times, there is also a Solar Swatch powered by sunlight and artificial light.

Swatch was appointed as Official Timekeeper to the Atlanta 1996 Olympic Games. Special collections of Swatches, beginning with the "Historical" and "Honor and Glory," and followed by two more, together with a limited-edition Chronometer model have been issued.

A special model has been designed, with the dial decorated with the logo of the Atlanta Olympic Games, and the strap at 6 o'clock bears the symbol of the British Olympic Team. The 12 o'clock strap carries the abbreviations of all 197 participating nations. There are two versions – gold for the athletes, silver for the fans. Part of the proceeds have gone to support Olympic teams, and the model is also on general sale.

LEFT
Pink Pleasure – appealing directly to the young.

BELOW
IRONY
"Scuba" – with leather strap, quartz movement and water-resistant to 655ft.

FLAGSHIP LINE

There is no flagship line as the designs are changed every year. All designs are in limited editions – up to 30,000 pieces – and are not repeated or carried over.

№46

Swiss Army Watches

Swiss Army watches were launched six years ago by the Forschner Group, who are also the distributors of the famous Victorinox Swiss Army knife which the company has been selling so successfully for more than thirty years.

ABOVE

OFFICERS

Officer's Two-tone, in gold and steel. Water-resistant to 330ft.

The Forschner Company originated in New Britain, Connecticut, in 1855 selling butcher's scales and other sundries which by the early 1930s included knives. They bought their knives from Victorinox, a Swiss firm which had been supplying knives to the Swiss Army since 1891. When the Forschner family sold out in 1957, the new owner decided to abandon the butcher's sundries side of the business and concentrate instead on the Swiss Army knives, of which Victorinox produced about 150 different versions.

Another change of ownership brought fresh ideas and enthusiasm. By the time the company went public in 1983, Swiss Army knives were a major part of the business and sales – now worldwide – had increased twelve-fold!

It seemed to the new proprietor that the qualities of durability, dependability, and fitness for purpose, together with Swiss engineering and good value for money which had contributed to the international success of Swiss Army knives, were the very virtues that would help to sell a similar product – namely a good Swiss watch.

Initially the line consisted of just three models in two sizes – large and small. Its features were rugged designs, uncluttered lines, and easy-to-read dials, driven by a reliable Swiss quartz movement. The first line was called the Original and it is still the bestselling line in the collection, which has now been extended to thirty different models spread over eight lines. The company's policy is keep the number of models small

RIGHT

STRIKER

Striking in yellow and black, with quartz movement and water-resistant to 300ft.

ABOVE

MILITARY

Unmistakable military look, quartz movement and water-resistant to 300ft.

PRODUCT RANGE

Original
Officers
Dual Time Zone
Cavalry
Chronograph
Renegade
Delta

BELOW
Officers comes in two sizes and in a choice of polished, black or red bezel, on a leather strap.

and to turn them over rapidly. Only a couple of new lines are introduced each year and then only to replace slow sellers.

All the wristwatches have Swiss quartz movements, with center seconds and a date indicator. The cases are in steel, polished or in alternative finishes, with mineral crystals and snap backs; all are water-protected, generally to 330 feet. The chronograph model, which is based on the Ronda 12-ligne 726-movement, has sub-dials for 30-minute and 12-hour elapsed time indicators and also for the date; it has a screwback and screwdown crown. All models carry a 12 month guarantee.

ABOVE
The individually tested and numbered Swiss Army Brand Chronograph, designed to communicate a wealth of vital, split-second information.

Apart from the Original, which comes in two sizes and three choices of bezel – black, red, and polished – there is the Officers, large or small, in polished stainless steel or two-tone finish on strap or bracelet. For those who want to be in two places at once, there is the Dual Time Zone, while for the nostalgic, the Cavalry's classic design might appeal. The Renegade is a chunky model that really looks as if it were made for the Swiss Army, especially in its olive drab case with matching Arnitel water-resistant strap.

FACT FILE

FOUNDED: 1978
COUNTRY OF ORIGIN: Switzerland
OUTPUT: 800,000 units worldwide per annum
MOVEMENT: All quartz models
CEO: Peter W. Gilson

BELOW
"ORIGINAL"

FLAGSHIP LINE

The Original model is still one of the bestsellers in the line, closely followed by the Officers line. In a way, the Swiss Army tag is the flagship.

№47

TAG-Heuer

Since its inception, TAG-Heuer has been associated with premier sporting events, a reputation in keeping with the aims of its 20-year-old founder Edouard Heuer, who started making chronographs for sportsmen as far back as 1860.

His workshop in Saint Imier was well-known for the precision and accuracy of his timers. In 1869 he patented a new stem-winding system; in 1886 he took out a patent for an improved pocket chronograph, and in 1880 a collection of his watches won a silver medal at the Paris Exposition.

PRODUCT RANGE

6000 Gold
6000 Series
4000 Series
2000 Series
1500 Series
S/E1 Collection
1964 Heuer Carrera

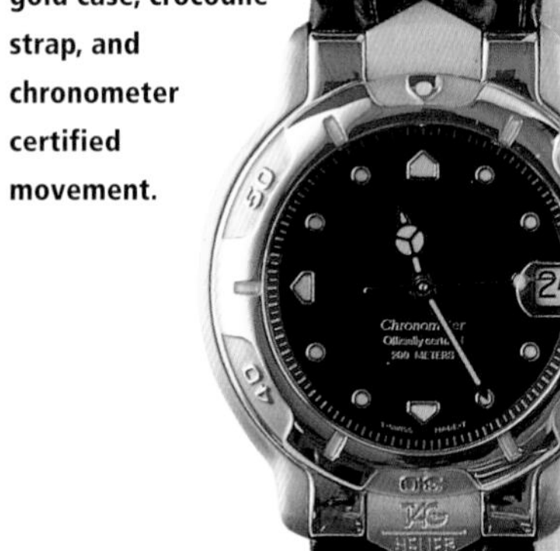

RIGHT
6000 SERIES "Auto", with 18kt gold case, crocodile strap, and chronometer certified movement.

The list of Heuer's achievements is formidable; the first timer with a 1/10th second-measuring capability (1916); official timekeeper to the Olympic Games in Antwerp (1920), Paris (1924), and Amsterdam (1928); invention of a flyback mechanism (1930), launch of an automotive instrument with interchangeable dials (1933).

The postwar progress of Heuer was equally impressive: the launch of the Solunar, a timing instrument showing tidal times (1949), and the design of the Chronosplit, the first double-display wristwatch quartz chronograph.

In the meantime, in 1974, Heuer had been appointed official timekeeper to the Ferrari Formula 1 Team, although it was not the firm's first association with motor racing. Jack Heuer, Edouard's grandson, developed a passion for motor racing in the 1950s. After competing initially himself, he took up timekeeping in the United States, in the course of which he learned about a 2,000-mile race across North America to the Guatemalan frontier. He was so impressed that in 1964 he persuaded his father Charles-Edouard to

ABOVE
SPORTS ELEGANCE Steel and gold plated case and bracelet. Chronometer certified automatic movement.

LEFT
2000 SERIES "Quartz", steel case and bracelet and sapphire glass.

ABOVE
The top-of-the line model in the 6000 series – 6000 Gold, automatic with date in solid 18kt gold.

produce a wrist chronograph and name it the Carrera. It was the first Heuer watch to bear a name and was an immediate success.

In 1980 Heuer was again appointed official timekeeper – this time to the Moscow Olympics; the Games were its last and ended a 60-year-old connection. Two years later, the Piaget group acquired an equity interest in the company, a move echoed in 1985 by its total acquisition by TAG (Techniques d'Avant Garde), a French company specializing in advanced technology. Henceforth, the company became TAG-Heuer.

The next year saw a return to Formula 1 Grand Prix racing. The company sponsored the successful Marlboro McLaren TAG Turbo in which Alain Prost won the world Driver's Championship and launched a Formula 1 sports watch in fiberglass and steel to commemorate the event.

In 1987 the firm developed a new line of electronic timing equipment to meet the critical demands of modern sports and launched a new line, the S/E1 Sports Elegance Collection. New collections of chronographs and chronometers, ever more precise, use all the technological advances in both quartz and mechanical horology, and the firm's prestige in this field was marked by its appointment as Official Timekeeper to the Formula 1 World Championship.

FACT FILE

FOUNDED: 1860
COUNTRY OF ORIGIN: Switzerland
OUTPUT: Switzerland's fifth largest producer
MOVEMENT: Mechanical, quartz
CEO: Christian Viros

TAG-Heuer's current collections include the 6000 series, of which the top-of-the-line model is the 6000 Gold, an automatic with date in solid 18-karat gold; there is a chronometer version, officially certified, in steel or steel and gold with a variety of dials, on a strap or bracelet. A lady's model in steel or bicolor is also available with mechanical automatic movement. The 6000 series can also be purchased with a quartz movement with center-seconds, date, and an end-of-battery-life indicator.

The S/E1 series includes a certified chronometer in a stylish case of steel or bicolor, its chunky look enhanced by a distinctive bracelet. This series, too, is available with quartz movements, including a lady's model in alternately polished and fine brushed steel. Top of this series is a mechanical automatic chronograph in a steel case, water-resistant to 660 feet. A choice of 1/10th or 1/100th-second timing is available.

BELOW
1964 Heuer Carrera in 18kt gold with silver dial and crocodile brown strap.

The S/E1 series also comes on water buffalo-hide straps with a folding buckle, and there is a choice of mechanical automatic or quartz movements.

TAG-Heuer also features a 4000 series of Sports watches fitted with mechanical automatic or quartz movements, on sharkskin straps or metal bracelets.

Then there is the 200 series, also available with mechanical or quartz movements, with gold-plated bezels and bracelet inserts which TAG-Heuer regards as its "starter" line for junior sportsmen and women, although there is an automatic 1/10th -second chronograph in the series which ranks with the best of them.

Finally, in descending numerical order comes the 1500 – all quartz, two sizes of steel case, water-resistant to 660 feet, with date and center-seconds.

The Formula 1 series – all quartz – has 1/10th-second chronographs and straight diver's models in synthetic cases. These watches have colored bezels and straps or smooth metal bracelets.

The latest model to join this impressive array of sports watches is the 1964 Heuer Carrera commemorative chronograph. Based on the original 1964 model introduced so passionately by Jack Heuer, it comes in stainless steel or 18-karat gold case with a mechanical chronograph movement; a flange on the rim of the dial angled at 30° provides a 1/5th-second scale. The dial – in black, white, or silver – is protected by a plexiglas watch glass – the same material as the original – and the model has a wider crown and larger pushpieces for easier operation when wearing driving gloves. (An open Ferrari or Porsche is envisaged.)

It is probably fair to say that TAG-Heuer provides the most comprehensive line of sports watches, from the relatively inexpensive to the wildly extravagant, of any manufacturer.

ABOVE
Series 4000 sports watches are fitted with mechanical automatic or quartz movements, on sharkskin straps or metal bracelets.

BELOW
2000 CHRONOGRAPH

FLAGSHIP LINE

TAG-Heuer's Series 2000 is the flagship line. Modestly priced, it epitomizes the company's attitude by combining function with style. It offers a wide choice of models, both quartz and mechanical, in two sizes, on strap or bracelet both with security clasp. Outstanding is the Chronograph.

№48

TIMEX

Timex is perhaps best known as a multibrand organization marketing more than 200 different models under its corporate umbrella. Split over 15 different names such as Wizards, Star Trek, and Essentials, all fall within a reasonable price bracket. The company is one of the world's leading watch manufacturers and has an impressive share of the important children's market; it is also prominent in licensing deals – with the Disney organization, the Guess group, and recently with Timberland, the American footwear company.

PRODUCT RANGE

Timex Datalink
Ironman
Mercury
Timberland

Typical of Timex's innovative production and styling is the Mercury. Originally introduced in 1959, it was still fashionable in 1995, by which time it had achieved almost cult status. Its movement contained only 75 moving parts, as opposed to the 100 of a typical quartz. Its simple clean case was water-protected, and the dial could be illuminated in the dark by Timex's own Indiglo system. Another bestselling style – Ironman – was claimed to be worn by President Bill Clinton – who presented one to the Smithsonian's National Museum of American History.

What has projected Timex into the forefront of technological horology is their recently launched Datalink, a watch that can be linked to a personal computer, provided it is loaded with Microsoft Windows 3.1 or higher, and a desktop monitor. The watch comes with its own software program developed by Timex in conjunction with Microsoft. Starting from information entered and stored on the PC, the wearer then selects entries to send to the watch, which can hold up to 70 items. A software memory sensor shows how much information has been selected. Transferring data from computer to watch is very easy. The Timex Datalink is pointed at the monitor, the screen

ABOVE
TIMEX DATALINK
Includes easy-to-use software to store up to 70 personal reminders.

RIGHT
TIMBERLAND
Rugged, high performance outdoor watch.

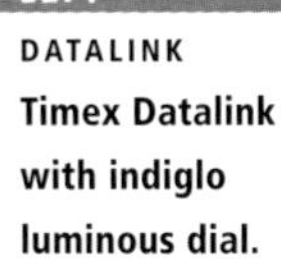

LEFT
DATALINK
Timex Datalink with indiglo luminous dial.

RIGHT

President Clinton donated his Timex Ironman Triathlon watch to the Smithsonian's National Museum of American History for a permanent exhibit featuring memorabilia from America's first families.

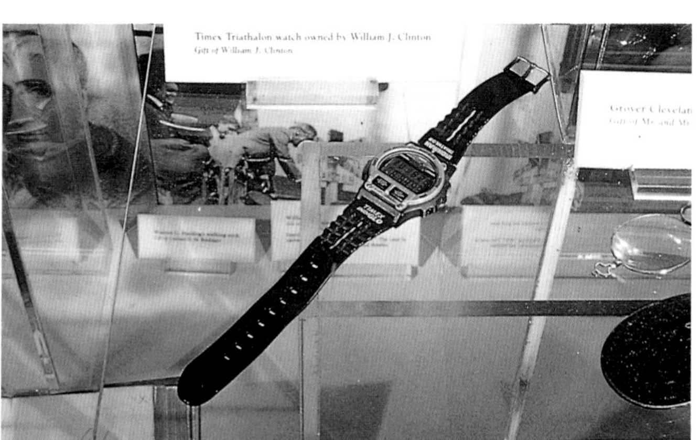

will display flashing bars of light, and a sensor in the watch reads the data. The Datalink also works with Microsoft Office for Windows 95.

The watch itself does not look very different from a normal complex LCD timepiece. It has dual time zones, 12- and 24-hour time formats, calendar, multiple alarms, hourly chimes, and a projected three-year battery life. It is lit in the dark by Timex's own Indiglo night light. The Datalink keeps the wearer's appointments and beeps to announce when it is time to leave for a meeting, and with whom, and where. It records phone numbers and addresses, recalled at the touch of a button; a reminder pops up a week before a preset anniversary or birthday; it stores confidential information such as access codes, locker combinations, PIN numbers; it can cope with up to five alarms a day, and ordinary time settings can be taken directly from the PC – two time zones can be entered, along with their international city codes.

ABOVE

Craftsmanship, superior durability and performance are all synonymous with the Timberland name. The watches are for men and women.

FACT FILE

FOUNDED: 1950
COUNTRY OF ORIGIN: United States
OUTPUT: 29 million units worldwide per annum
MOVEMENT: Quartz
CEO: Mike Jacobi

The Timex Datalink comes in a variety of case styles water-protected, depending on the case, from 100 to 330 feet. The latest model 150 with "Wrist Apps" allows the wearer to add more functions such as a countdown timer and a 31-character scrolling message line, and doubles the memory storage to 150 entries.

BELOW

MERCURY

FLAGSHIP LINE

One of Timex's most popular normal models is the Mercury, originally launched in 1959 and relaunched in 1995 with the addition of an Indiglo night light. Timex's current outstanding innovation is the Datalink.

Nº49

TISSOT

Tissot is the leading name in SMH's mid-priced watches, accounting for over half the sales in this sector, the others being Certina, Pierre Balmain, Hamilton, and Mido. It had its origins in 1853 when Charles-Emile Tissot returned to Le Locle after working in America for five years and persuaded his father Charles-Félicien to open a watch factory. Their watches were sold to dealers in the United States and then to Russia, a market which Charles-Emile particularly cultivated and which became their biggest customer up to the Revolution in 1917. In 1904 the Russian court gave them an order for a pocket watch to be awarded to officers for special services.

The first Tissot wristwatch was produced in 1915, and in 1919 they created the Banana watch – a gold Art Deco wristwatch which curved around the wrist. In 1920 the firm started to mass produce watches with the introduction of the Knoplock watch, and also produced a silver pocket watch with an alarm.

Tissot broke new ground with the first antimagnetic watch in 1930 and in 1944 came the first fully automatic watch, the PR 500, designed by Paul Tissot, the founder's grandson. The Tissot Navigator (1953) was the first automatic watch with an international calendar which could display world as well as local time, and by 1956 this was refined into the PR 516, an automatic, antimagnetic watch with calendar in a case water-resistant to 330 feet. Meanwhile, Tissot, which had been operated up to this time as a family firm, merged in 1930 with Omega to form SSIH in a move to strengthen its international presence. Fifty years later, after the fusion of SSIH and ASUAG, Tissot became a subsidiary of SMH, and once again was in a position to operate independently within the overall SMH umbrella.

Tissot ushered in the new electronic age by developing a new magnetic clutch which facilitates accurate automatic time zone changes. They also produced the Chrono Quartz multifunction quartz chronograph with both analog

ABOVE
PR 100
Automatic movement. When fully wound has a power reserve lasting approximately 42 hours.

PRODUCT RANGE

Rock Watch
Woodwatch
PR 50 Chrono
PR 100
PR 100 Diver
Navigator
Ceraton

TISSOT

BELOW
PR 100 DIVER
Water-resistant to 330ft, quartz movement.

ABOVE
PR 50 CHRONO
With three basic functions: stop/start, rally and split function.

FACT FILE

FOUNDED: 1853
COUNTRY OF ORIGIN: Switzerland
OUTPUT: Information not available
MOVEMENT: Mechanical, quartz
CEO: Nicholas Hayek

and digital display. A further development was the Two-Timer, also with two display modes. In its introduction the use of computer-controlled machines reduced both the cost of production and the number of parts, with the backplate of the watch eventually forming part of its case.

In 1985 Tissot launched its first Rock Watch – another of Dr. Thomke's inventions, it is said – in which the case was made of Swiss granite millions of years old. Milled from different quarries, no two pieces are the same, and the rock-like material includes topaz, garnet, tourmaline, and pyrites that give a sparkling effect in certain lights. In a further development, the "Jewels of Nature" series had faces of semiprecious stones, mother-of-pearl, coral, and shell.

In 1980 Woodwatch was introduced, its unusual case carved from Corsican briar, a wood that has traditionally been used for making tobacco pipes, and in 1991 Tissot added the ceramic Ceraton watch to the collection.

ABOVE
Tissot Ballade Chrono, water-resistant to 100ft with scratch-resistant sapphire crystal, and leather strap.

Many of these unique watches have found their way into collectors' hands. Conventional timepieces have not been ignored, however, demonstrated by the recent launch of the PR 50, a quartz chronograph with all the normal functions, split times, and an end-of-battery-life indicator. The company has also reissued the Navigator, a classic replica of the 1950s model with mechanical automatic movement in a gold-plated case with a Hesalite crystal.

RIGHT
The multifunctional Tissot 7 includes date and day of the week in English, French or Spanish. All seven functions are in 12 or 24 hour mode.

BELOW
ROCK WATCH

FLAGSHIP LINE

The Rock Watch must be regarded as Tissot's flagship line. Although it is now ten years old, it is still a favorite with customers.

№50
Ulysse Nardin

The headquarters of Ulysse Nardin is in Le Locle, high in the Jura Mountains northwest of Neuchâtel, where in 1774 Jean-Léonard Nardin set up a business making stoves and other domestic implements. His son Léonard-Frédéric developed an interest in watchmaking and laid the foundations of a famous watchmaking dynasty.

Ulysse Nardin, Léonard Frédéric's son, was just 24 when, in 1846, he started a company to make marine chronometers and alarm watches. His timepieces soon won international recognition, culminating in the coveted Prize Medal at the 1862 World's Fair in London.

RIGHT
ASTROLABIUM GALILEO GALILEI
In 18kt gold case. The dial can be ordered for any latitude.

In 1876 his son Paul-David Nardin took over the company. His products were bought by 60 shipping companies and won a remarkable 4,800 official awards and prizes. After his death in 1920, for the next 25 years the company was run by his three sons. However, having established a new line of extra-thin automatic watches, Ulysse Nardin faced the economic crisis of the 1970s and the inexorable advance of quartz technology.

BELOW
PLANETARIUM COPERNICUS
The planet rings of this Limited Edition are cut from a meteorite found in 1896 in Greenland.

In 1983 a small group of investors under the direction of Rolf Schnyder took over the company and gave it a period of tranquility while stocks were rationalized and the retail network overhauled. Schnyder had worked for Jaeger-LeCoultre and had become a successful industrialist in Hong Kong. He was determined to restore the company to its former eminences and enlisted the support of Dr. Ludwig Oechstin, an astronomer and mathematician who also had an interest in watchmaking, and had built a three-foot astrolabe which was seen by Schnyder in Lucerne. It gave him an idea.

PRODUCT RANGE

Astrolabium Galileo Galilei
Planetarium Copernicus
Marine Chronometer 1846
Michelangelo
GMT±
San Marco Chronometer

The Astrolabium Galileo Galilei was a unique astrolabe, created as a tribute to its namesake. Unveiled at the 1985 Basel Fair, it took the horological world by storm. Its automatic movement was only 9mm thick and its diameter was 30mm. It was the first wristwatch to offer, in

LEFT
TELLURIUM
Complete with map and signs of the zodiac.

addition to the time of day, local time, and month, a number of astronomical indications such as the height and direction of the sun, moon, and stars; moonphases and eclipses of the sun and moon; and the signs of the Zodiac. Its five hands, all on the same axis, turn at different speeds. It was so complicated that Schnyder had to write a book of operating instructions.

ABOVE

Ulysse Nardin was an astute business man. He saw a "gap in the market" and moved into the manufacture of marine chronometers.

This *tour de force* was followed in 1988 by the Planetarium Copernicus, a timepiece that displays the solar system with the planets Mercury, Venus, Mars, Jupiter, and Saturn. It was created as a tribute to the East Prussian scientist Nicolaus Copernicus (1473–1543), whose theory that the planets, including the Earth, moved around the sun enraged the Church. Ulysse Nardin's Trilogy of Time was completed with the introduction in 1992 of the Tellurium. This extraordinary wristwatch has in the center of its dial a projection of the earth in its true geographic perspective as seen from the North Pole. Apart from telling the time, it has a perpetual calendar, and the time and place of the rising and setting of the sun, as well as many other astronomical details. In addition to producing these unique pieces, the company continued to manufacture about 40 different mechanical timepieces, including wristwatch minute repeaters, tourbillon chronometer regulators with separate hour and minute indicators, including the popular Michelangelo 18-karat gold rectangular wristwatch with mechanical movement which indicated day, date, month, and moonphase.

FACT FILE

FOUNDED: 1846
COUNTRY OF ORIGIN: Switzerland
OUTPUT: Approximately 4,000 per annum
MOVEMENT: Mechanical
CEO: Rolf Schnyder

To mark its 150th anniversary, Ulysse Nardin launched a Marine Chronometer 1846 wristwatch, in a limited edition in yellow, pink, and white gold, with an enamel dial and water-resistance to 660 feet. It has a characteristic oversized seconds hand display and has a 42-hour power reserve. All models carry an official chronometer certificate.

Another of Ludwig Oechstin's contributions to Ulysse Nardin was the design of its GMT± world timer. The problem was to find a way of changing the hours when passing from East to West or vice-versa without changing the timing of the minutes. Using the crown meant removing the watch from the wrist. Oechstin solved the problem by means of a unique mechanism, which means the change can be made in full hours by pressing a button at 8 o'clock. The GMT± is now the company's bestselling line.

RIGHT

GMT± WORLD TIMER

FLAGSHIP LINE

The GMT± World Timer comes in a variety of cases from steel on strap to 18-karat gold on a bracelet.

№51

UNIVERSAL GENEVE

Universal Genève was founded in 1894 by Georges Perret, who was joined three years later by Louis Berthoud. They were originally wholesalers and distributors for other manufacturers, but by the turn of the century had begun to sell watches themselves. It was not until 1934, however, that they decided the firm should have its own brand and registered the name "Universal."

PRODUCT RANGE

Golden Janus
Golden Tech
Golden Mastertech
Golden Chronotech
Golden Computech
Golden Tech Diver
Golden Tradition
Golden Country Club

Like many of their contemporaries, they bought in parts and assembled them to their own standards in their small factory. When Perret's son Raoul joined the firm, he introduced a touch of elegance into the designs. After World War I, the company produced its first wrist chronograph which it called the Universal Watch Extra, and throughout the 1930s it created a number of Compur models, including a lady's chronograph. In 1936 came the well-known Compax models which included AeroCompax (1940), DateCompax, MedicoCompax, and TriCompax (1944), one of the first to indicate moonphase and one of the company's most popular models.

From 1952–57 the company registered five important patents including the Microtor, an automatic with the winding rotor set into the movement instead of on top, which led to the production of the thinnest automatic movement in the world at that time.

In 1954 the company moved its factory to Carouge, on the outskirts of Geneva. No doubt the proximity of the home of Swiss watchmaking inspired them to add its name. It was now known as Universal Genève.

1954 also saw the launch of the Polerouter, chosen by Scandinavian Airlines for its inaugural flight over the North Pole, and in 1966 the company's Golden Shadow models won a number of prestigious international awards including the

ABOVE
GOLDEN TRADITION
A classic watch with mechanical movement, in 18kt gold case.

BELOW
GOLDEN CHRONOTECH
With automatic movement, here in stainless steel case and bracelet.

LEFT
GOLDEN JANUS
Created as a celebration of the company's jubilee.

Golden Rose of Baden Baden. This was to be their heyday. The problems of the 1970s and the onset of electronics proved too much and in 1986 Universal Genève was taken over by Stelux, a Hong Kong-based group of investors headed by Joseph Wong.

New strategies, new product lines, and new distribution agreements have restored this old-established company, and to mark its centenary in 1994, Universal Genève launched a unique timepiece.

The Janus watch has two dials, one on each side, which show the time in two time zones. There is only one movement, the well-known UG42 manually wound caliber just 3.8mm thick. On the conventional (i.e. front) dial, leaf hands indicate hours and minutes; on the back dial, jumping hours are shown in a window at 12 o'clock, while a leaf hand points to the minutes. Date and day or night time are indicated by subsidiary dials. The functions are synchronized and can be set together by the single crown at 3 o'clock or individually by two other crowns at 8 and 10 o'clock.

ABOVE
Golden Janus has back-to-back dials. One shows hours and minutes, the other a second time-zone in jumping hours.

The case is in two parts, with one external platinum unit enclosing a second element fitted with a device which allows it to be turned over. A lever at 6 o'clock locks the movement of the case. The limited-edition Golden Janus is available in 18-karat gold or platinum on a leather strap.

FACT FILE

FOUNDED: 1894
COUNTRY OF ORIGIN: Switzerland
OUTPUT: Information not available
MOVEMENT: Mechanical
CEO: William J. G. Devine

Under the "Golden" banner, Universal Genève has issued a number of collections with modern styling but more than a touch of the traditional designs for which it was so well known in the 1960s. These include Golden Tech, with automatic movement; Golden Master Tech, with split seconds chronograph and power reserve indicator; Golden Arrow Tech, with automatic chronograph movement with a date window; Golden Computech, another automatic chronograph with day date; and Golden Tech Diver, an automatic in a case water-resistant to 330 feet. All these models come in 18-karat gold or stainless-steel cases, with sapphire crystals and a choice of dial finishes, and some are available in smaller cases.

The Golden Tradition Classic line has mechanical movements, in 18-karat gold cases.

Golden Country Club is a less expensive collection, in three sizes of case, in stainless steel or 18-karat gold and steel combination with an automatic or quartz movement.

FLAGSHIP LINE

The Golden Tech in all its variations.

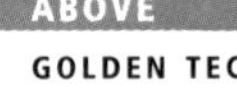

ABOVE
GOLDEN TECH

№52

Vacheron Constantin

Vacheron Constantin claims to be the oldest watch manufacturer in the world, having been in uninterrupted production since 1755, when 24-year-old Jean-Marc Vacheron set up his workshop in Geneva.

For the next 30 years, he built up a reputation for making watches of the highest quality. He trained apprentices and taught other watchmakers, including his son Abraham to whom he handed over the business in 1785.

The end of the century saw a difficult time. Napoleon's army was at the city's gates; they press-ganged his apprentices and scared away his customers. Abraham gave up and relinquished the firm to his son Barthélemy. Helped financially by his father-in-law, Barthélemy built up the firm's fortunes but found the necessary traveling rather tedious. A family friend took it off his hands; François Constantin was a bit of a rake but a shrewd businessman; he traveled all over Europe – often at considerable risk – to get orders and deliver the goods.

To meet the demand, the partners took on a mechanical genius named Lechot who designed and built a range of precision machines which revolutionized production without sacrificing the quality for which the firm was by now renowned. It was about this time that the company registered the Maltese Cross as its trademark. By the 1900s the factory, now established at its present address, began producing the newly developed wristwatches, receiving orders from the American forces.

In the 1920s, the company made its first Grande Complication, a minute repeater with split seconds chronograph, perpetual calendar, moonphase, and alarm, but it concentrated on making high-quality timepieces for normal use. The 200th anniversary was celebrated with a man's mechanical movement a mere 1.64mm high – a record, followed by the world's thinnest automatic with a height of only 2.45mm. But concentration on these technical achievements took attention off the market, and by the time the present chief

RIGHT
LES HISTORIQUES
A more classic look. Platinum with leather strap and silvered index dial.

ABOVE
MERCATOR
In 18kt gold case and dial, representing Europe, Africa and Asia. A homage to Gerardus Mercator, father of modern cartography.

LEFT
LES COMPLICATIONS
18kt gold with silver index dial and leather strap.

PRODUCT RANGE

Phideas
Les Historiques
Les Absolues
Les Complications
Les Essentials

VACHERON CONSTANTIN

LEFT
Kalla Amalfi, typical of the "Les Absolues," in 18kt white gold case set with baguette-cut diamonds.

executive took over, the firm had a splendid reputation but a sparse retail network and considerable obsolete stock. Claude-Daniel Proellochs restored the firm's fortunes so successfully that within five years production had trebled to 10,000 pieces annually.

FACT FILE

FOUNDED: 1755
COUNTRY OF ORIGIN: Switzerland
OUTPUT: 10,000 units per annum
MOVEMENT: Men's 90% mechanical, ladies' 60% mechanical
CEO: Claude-Daniel Proellochs

The present line contains about 100 models spread over five major collections.

Phideas is the flagship line, classic designs in 18-karat gold cases on matching bracelets with automatic movements. Les Historiques reflect the traditional design of the past; typical is the Jalousie, inspired by a 1930s model. It has a unique system of shutters which cover the dial and can be opened and closed by means of a slide set with a cabochon sapphire. Its rectangular 18-karat pink-gold case sets off the white gold of the shutters. It has a handwound mechanical movement.

Les Absolues pay homage to the jeweler's art; emblazoned with diamonds and precious stones, they also tell the time. Typical is the Kalla Amalfi in an 18-karat white-gold case set with baguette-cut diamonds. They have manually wound mechanical movements and come in two sizes – women's and men's.

Les Complications display all the technical skills of the company's master watchmaker; an interesting example is the Jumping Hour manually wound model in 18-karat gold on a strap.

Les Essentials are a collection of round gold-cased models on a strap; in any lesser brand it might be called the lead-in line.

BELOW
1928 Grand Complication pocket watch in 18kt gold with perpetual calendar, moon phases in lapiz lapuli, minute-repeater with chimes, alarm, and split second chronograph movement.

BELOW
Sovereign is a new 18kt pink gold line with a particularly attractive and original bracelet.

ABOVE
Jalousie has a unique system of shutters that cover the dial.

RIGHT
Painting by François de Ziegler of an 18th century Cabinotier's workshop. Watchmakers were known as Cabinotiers because of the small size of their premises, almost like cabins.

To mark its 240th anniversary, Vacheron Constantin launched a commemorative watch called the 240 in 18-karat pink gold with self-winding movement, power-reserve indicator, and a pointer-type date hand. Only 5 individually numbered pieces were produced. The back bears an engraving of Geneva's Tour de I'lle, symbol of the watchmaking district where the company first had its premises.

Another singular model was the Mercator, designed in homage to the master cartographer. In 18-karat gold it had a gold dial, hand-chased to represent one of Mercator's maps, and a self-winding mechanical movement. The watch features retrograde hands, like a pair of compasses, which displayed the hours and minutes in an arc. It was produced in a limited edition of 1,000 pieces. Vacheron Constantin is one of the few remaining manufacturers who make all their own movements and parts and assemble them in their own factories.

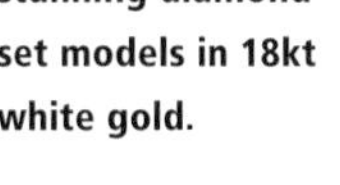

RIGHT
Les Tonneaux – stunning diamond-set models in 18kt white gold.

FLAGSHIP LINE

The Phideas line of classical designs on 18-karat gold cases on bracelets, with Vacheron Constantin's own automatic movements.

RIGHT
PHIDEAS

№53

Yves St. Laurent

What makes a successful couturier want to get into the watch business?

Yves St. Laurent was born in Oran in Algeria in 1936 and in 1953, at the age of 17, won a prize for the design of a cocktail dress. By 1958 he had become the artistic director of Christian Dior following the founder's death. In 1961 he created his own *maison de couture* and two years later presented his first collection. He added jewelry, perfume, and other products to complete the effect.

Four years later, he opened his first *prêt à porter* boutique, which by 1969 had grown to over 100 shops worldwide. The Cartier Group took a part of the Yves St. Laurent Group when the latter, which by then also included Charles of the Ritz, came on the stock market. The YSL Group was subsequently bought by Sanofi, a subsidiary of the ELF Group, in 1993.

FACT FILE

FOUNDED: 1969
COUNTRY OF ORIGIN: France
OUTPUT: Information not available
MOVEMENT: Quartz
CEO: Pierre Bergé

PRODUCT RANGE

Majorelle
Love series
Lear
Bamako

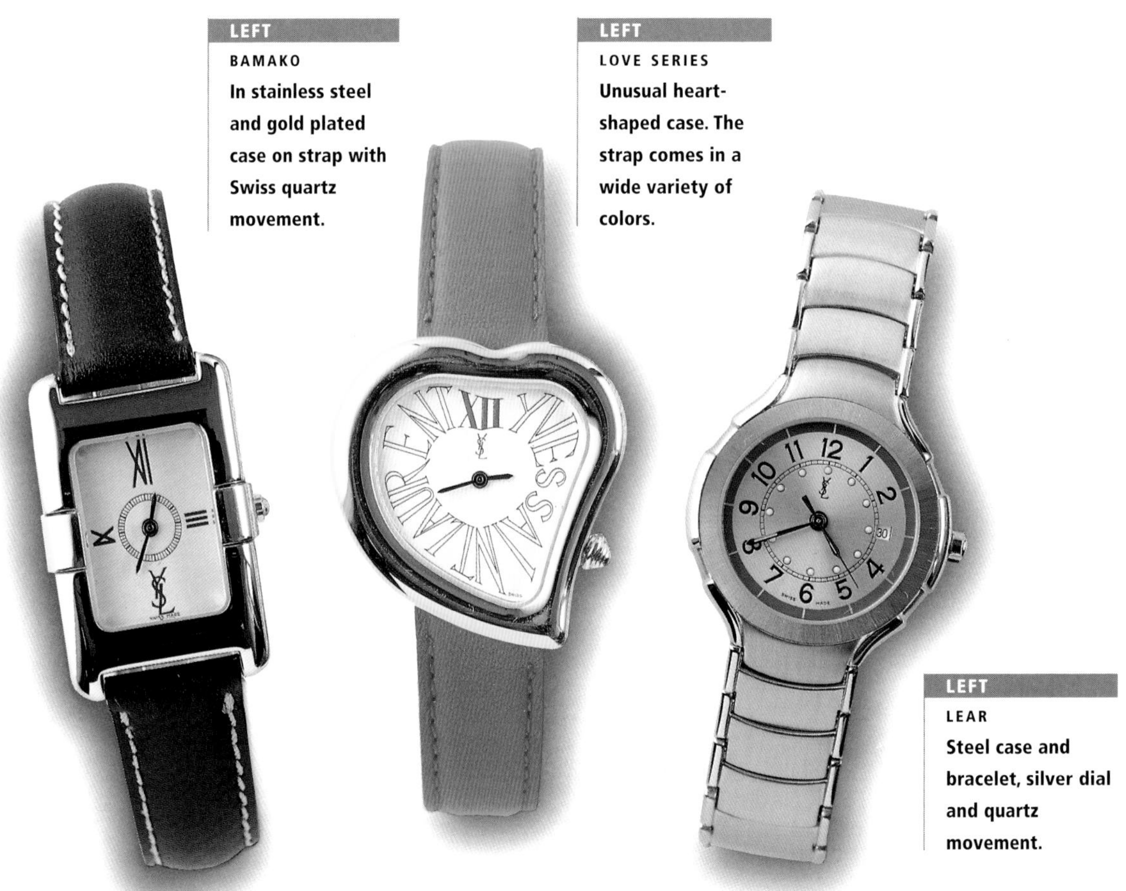

LEFT
BAMAKO
In stainless steel and gold plated case on strap with Swiss quartz movement.

LEFT
LOVE SERIES
Unusual heart-shaped case. The strap comes in a wide variety of colors.

LEFT
LEAR
Steel case and bracelet, silver dial and quartz movement.

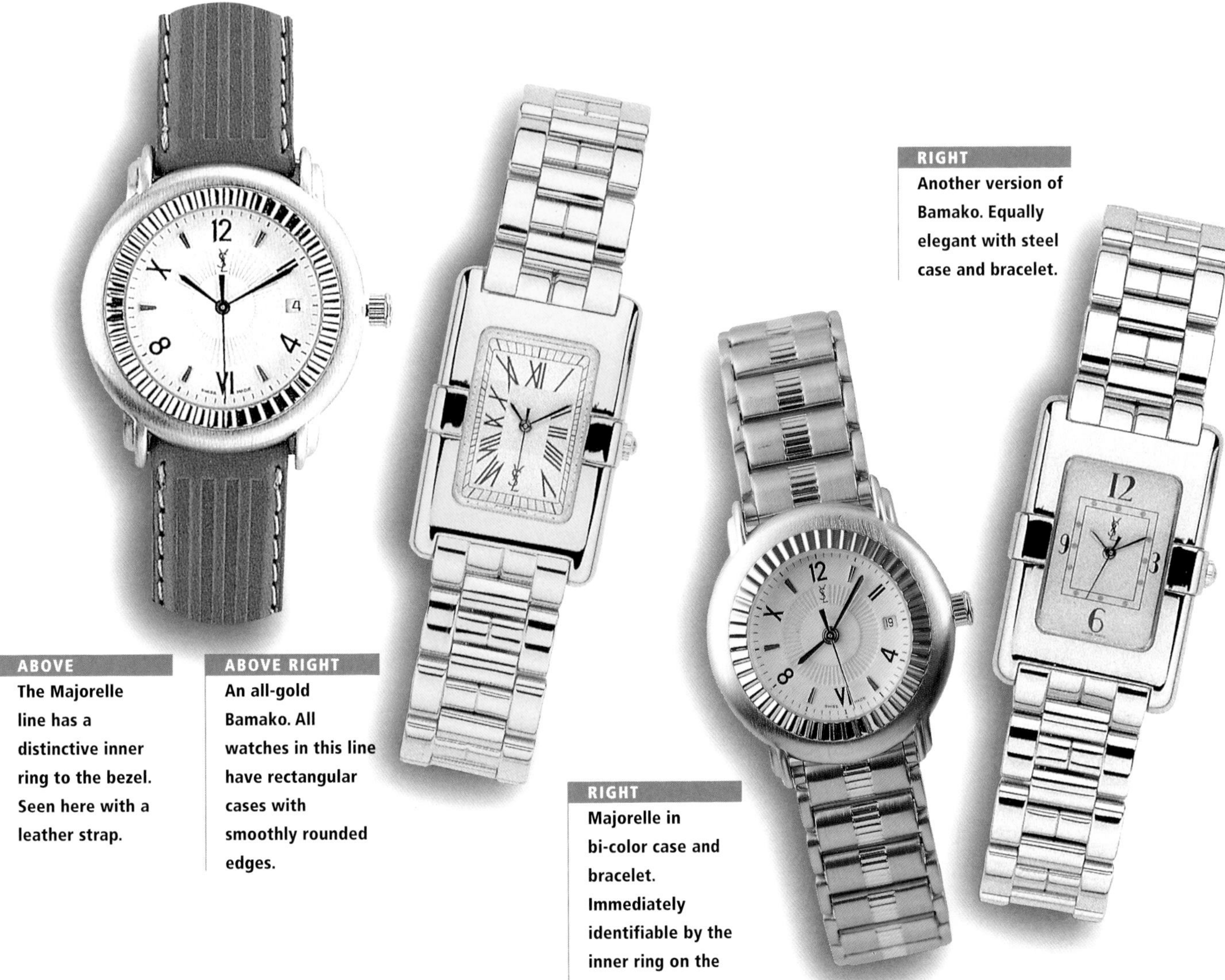

ABOVE
The Majorelle line has a distinctive inner ring to the bezel. Seen here with a leather strap.

ABOVE RIGHT
An all-gold Bamako. All watches in this line have rectangular cases with smoothly rounded edges.

RIGHT
Majorelle in bi-color case and bracelet. Immediately identifiable by the inner ring on the bezel.

RIGHT
Another version of Bamako. Equally elegant with steel case and bracelet.

The Cartier connection obviously introduced watches into the YSL scene. Its current lines include the Love series, in palladium or gold plate on straps of varying colors or bracelets matching the unusual outline. The Majorelle line is the most popular; the round models have a distinctive inner ring to the bezel. The Lear collection also has round cases which extend into the strap or bracelets, while the Bamako models have rectangular cases with smoothly rounded edges. All YSL models come in gold-plated or palladium-finished cases, with a choice of straps or matching bracelets.

FLAGSHIP LINE

Majorelle is YSL's flagship line.

RIGHT
MAJORELLE

№54

ZENITH

From its very beginnings, Zenith has been a little different from the conventional watch-producing house. To start with, when its founder Georges Favre-Jacot opened his Fabrique de Billodes in Le Locle in 1865, he decided to go straight into the production of complete watches, using up-to-date machinery and tools which he designed and made himself.

His first models were pocket watches, and he coined the name Zenith for them. He was a fanatic for quality, and Zenith represented the ultimate – the nearest one could get to perfection. One of his watches earned him a Grand Prix at the Universal Exhibition in Paris in 1900, the first of more than 1,500 such awards.

RIGHT
CLASS 6
Elegant and classic, Class 6 watches are ultraslim.

Georges also went into production with "Neuchâtel" clocks, which gained a considerable share of the market. He went quickly into the manufacture of the newly invented wristwatches, and their success led to the formation of a joint stock company, Fabriques de Montres Zenith, in 1911, with a subsidiary company in London set up in 1914 to distribute the company's products in the U.K.

ABOVE
DEFY
Bicolor case and bracelet, sapphire glass and undirectional rotating bezel.

For the next fifty years, Zenith continued to produce a collection of watches for an increasingly international clientele. As one of the few genuine *manufactures*, the firm made not only all its own movements and parts, but supplied some of the other top Swiss brands as well.

RIGHT
RAINBOW
Gold automatic chronograph equipped with the legendary "El Primero" movement.

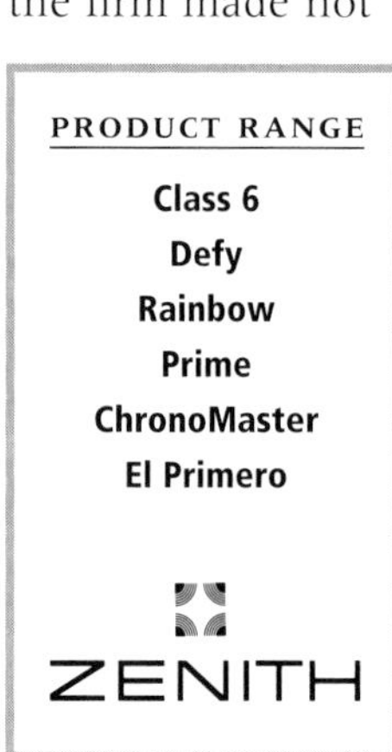

Shortly after the firm's centenary, Zenith engineers came up with a revolutionary new design, the first self-winding movement, with a 36,000 vph fast beat capable of timing to 1/10th second over short periods. Called El Primero, it took two years to perfect and was launched at the 1969 Basel Fair.

About this time Zenith acquired two other well-known Swiss companies, Mondia and Movado, but scarcely had the new group begun operations than the Zenith Radio Corporation of Chicago acquired a majority shareholding. They immediately introduced the new quartz technology in Zenith's brands, which resulted in the launch of the Futura containing analog and digital displays in an

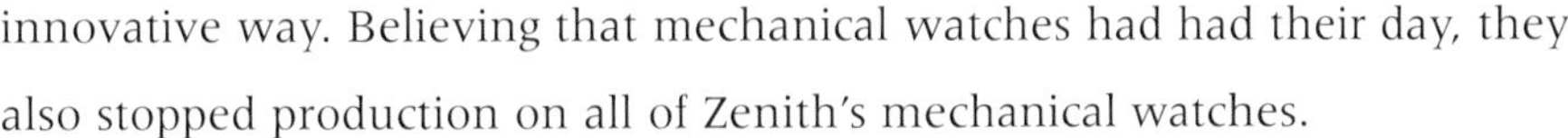

BELOW
El Primero Chronograph – a cornerstone of Zenith's collection.

innovative way. Believing that mechanical watches had had their day, they also stopped production on all of Zenith's mechanical watches.

Fortunately, one of the firm's engineers hung onto the tools and drawings of El Primero for safe keeping. In 1978, the American amalgamation failed, and the company was acquired by Paul Castella, a Swiss businessman and head of the international Dixi group of Le Locle. Under Swiss management again, the tools were brought back, and El Primero was once again in the stock; it has been a cornerstone of the company's collection since.

RIGHT
El Primero Automatic – part of the Rainbow Collection.

Zenith now settled down once again to produce high-quality watches, both mechanical and quartz. In 1990 to mark the 150th anniversary, the company launched limited editions of two certified chronometers: the following year, two more were added. Then in 1994 came the introduction of the Series 6. It was fitted with an automatic movement with the quality of El Primero, but with different characteristics. Designed and developed in house, the Elite movement took four years and a considerable investment in computer technology and was the company's first completely new movement for twenty-five years. In 1995 it was awarded the "Best Mechanical Movement of the Year."

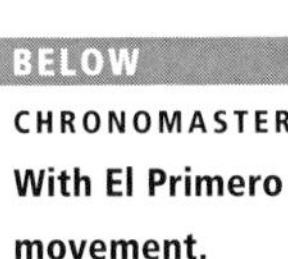

BELOW
CHRONOMASTER
With El Primero movement.

Originally launched in limited editions in gold or platinum, Class 6 (as it is now known) uses three versions of Zenith's Elite 11½-ligne ultraslim self-winding movement. The 610 has sweep seconds hand and date; the 680 also has the date, with small seconds at 9 o'clock. Both are used on the Classic City models; and the 682, with small seconds, date, and second time-zone indicator, is used in the three models of the Sports collection. All are available in steel or steel and gold, each collection has a choice of three dials, and the City models have see-through backs. The cases are water-resistant to 100 feet, and all models are on Louisiana crocodile straps.

FACT FILE

FOUNDED: 1865
COUNTRY OF ORIGIN: Switzerland
OUTPUT: Information not available
MOVEMENT: Mechanical 40% in volume, 70% in value
CEO: François Manfredini

FLAGSHIP LINE

The Class 6 automatic watch with the Elite movement is a star performer in Zenith's collection, rivaled only by the ChronoMaster, a chronograph with chronometer performance using the El Primero movement.

N°55

Zodiac

The trade name Zodiac was first registered in 1908, although it had already been used for many years by a dynasty of watchmakers by the name of Calame in Le Locle.

There is a record of a Jacob Calame, watchmaker-farmer in 1820, and of his son Julien who carried on the craft in St. Imier, but the history of the company begins in 1864 when Ariste Calame, after an apprenticeship to an assembler, set up a small workshop in Crêt-Vaillant which he soon turned into a watch trading house whence he supplied many well-known watchmaking companies with watches.

Ariste handed over a solid if unspectacular business to his son Louis-Ariste in 1900. With the enthusiasm of the young Louis, 25 and newly wed, gave up supplying watches as an *établisseur* and became an exporter in his own right, finding a particular market in Japan where his watches were distributed by Hattori-Seiko.

His success meant a move to larger premises in 1908, where the firm remained until 1950; he turned the company into a *manufacture,* making all his own parts and the tools as well, and he registered the name Zodiac. For the next twenty years, the company steadily built up its connections; Louis was one of the founders of the Federation of the Associations of Watchmakers, now known as the FH. In 1923 he was joined by his son René Calame, already trained as a watchmaker and technician. He turned the business into a limited company, which helped it survive the crises of the 1930s and World War II.

By 1945 the business had grown to such an extent that René's brother Maurice was brought in as commercial director. Once again the firm had to move to larger premises in Le Locle; by 1966 it had to expand further, building an extension to the earlier premises.

In 1978 Pierre Calame, the latest member of the family to be chief executive, recognized that a turning point had been reached, not just in Zodiac's case, but in the Swiss watch industry as

PRODUCT LINE

Marine Life
Seawolf Chronograph
Gold Point Fixed Bezel
Gold Point Quartz
Swiss Formula

ABOVE
SWISS FORMULA
With satinized stainless steel case, phosphorescent dial and green calf-lined sharkskin strap.

RIGHT
SILVER POINT 11 COLLECTION
Stainless steel case and bracelet and blue dial. Water-resistant to 660ft.

BELOW
SEAWOLF CHRONOGRAPH
With stainless steel case and midnight blue leather strap. Water-resistant to 330ft.

ABOVE
From the Silver Point II Collection, with stainless steel case and bracelet, white dial and quartz movement with calendar.

a whole. Faced with the all-too-familiar story of lack of financial resources, the firm was saved by Paul Castella, the Swiss businessman who had already rescued Zenith from its American owner. In 1981, the company was initially merged with Zenith, whose factory at Le Locle currently produces Zodiac watches.

During its independent years, Zodiac had in 1924 launched an extra-flat pocket watch; it had been one of the first Swiss companies to produce automatic watches; in 1932 Zodiac invented the Autographic power reserve indicator system (now a collector's piece), and in the same year it perfected a modern shock-resist system.

Its postwar activities included the launch of Seawolf, a professional diver's watch, and in 1968 the Dynatron, one of the first Swiss electronic watches. In 1970 it helped launch the first Swiss analog quartz watch, using the famous Beta 21 caliber and in 1977 the first LCD watch to obtain an official chronometer certificate. It also claimed to produce, in 1978, the world's slimmest quartz and the flattest automatic watch with calendar.

BELOW
Seawolf in two-tone, with a sparkling fluted and polished fixed bezel.

In recent years its collection has increased to some 250 models, including the Gold Point Fixed Bezel in stainless steel with an ETA quartz movement with date. The back and crown are screwed; it is water-protected to 660 feet. It is available in three sizes and in two-tone steel and gold plate or all gold plated.

FACT FILE
FOUNDED: 1864
COUNTRY OF ORIGIN: Switzerland
OUTPUT: 50,000 pieces per annum
MOVEMENT: Mechanical, quartz
CEO: Willy Gad Monnier

The Seawolf Automatic Chronograph has a Valjou 7750 movement with a 40-hour power reserve, unidirectional rotating bezel partially gold-plated in a stainless steel case. Water resistant to 330 feet, it comes in just one size, but three choices of finish. The luminous dial has a tachymeter track. Latest is the Marine Life with an ETA quartz chronograph movement, with split seconds unidirectional turning bezel, screwback, sapphire glass, stainless steel or two-tone steel and gold-plated case, water-resistant to 660 feet, on a matching bracelet.

These models are very much in keeping with the sporting image for which the brand is known and in which field its present chief executive, Willy Gad Monnier, who took over in 1989, has considerable international experience.

FLAGSHIP LINE

Zodaic say they do not have a flagship line. In 1996 it concentrated on the Chrono Marine Life.

RIGHT
CHRONO MARINE LIFE

GLOSSARY

analogue indicating time and information by means of hands on a dial.
antimagnetic Protected from magnetism; should meet ISO Standard. Quartz watches are not usually affected by magnetism.
applied numerals (appliqué) Raised metal numbers or batons attached to dial by adhesion or pegs.
arbor Horological name for an axle, usually with a toothed wheel attached to it.
Art Deco Design style of the 1920–30s.
automatic watch Mechanical watch with a mainspring that is wound by means of a rotor which is activated by the wearer's movements.
auxiliary dial, or bottom or subsidiary dial Small dial to show additional information, which is especially on chronographs.
back plate The base of the movement.
balance Basically, an oscillator which regulates or governs the speed of the movement. A flat ring which pivots on an axle. It must be perfectly poised. After it has swung one way, the spring at its center reverses it and makes it swing the other way – hence the "tick tock" of a mechanical watch. Both balance and hairspring are made of a special alloy to offset the effect of temperature changes.
balance staff The axle on which the balance pivots.
beat The vibration (half oscillation) of a movement – i.e. the number of ticks.
bridge Metal plates that hold pivots or jewels in place in the movement.
bezel Metal plates that hold pivots or jewels In place in the movement.
bubble back Term sometimes used for certain mechanical watches with a deep, curved back.
cabochon Decorative stone set in winding crown.
caliber Used to denote the size of a movement usually measured in lignes (2.256mm); also used by manufacturers as "names" for their movements.
center or sweep seconds Seconds hand positioned at the center of the dial indicating seconds at edge of the main dial.
chapter ring Circle bearing the hour (and sometimes minute) numerals or marks.
chronograph Watch which has an independent stop mechanism for short interval timing.
chronometer Watch which has gained an Official Timing Certificate after reliability tests by the official Swiss authority.
complication Watch with more functions than just the time of day (e.g. alarm, moonphase, perpetual calendar, power reserve indicator, split seconds, repeater). The term is usually used only for mechanical watches.
crown Knob usually at 3 o'clock, for winding and setting the hands, and date where fitted.
crystal Cover made of glass, plastic, or synthetic sapphire, fitted with a bezel. Sometimes referred to as a "glass," it is made from.
date window Opening in dial showing date no matter what and sometimes the month and/or day of the week.
dial The face of a watch, showing hours, minutes, and seconds. Other small dials are auxiliary or subsidiary.
digital watch Indicates time by numerical display.
ebauche Literally a frame; commonly used for an unassembled movement, without escapement, balance and hairspring, and mainspring.
escape wheel Last wheel in going train, working with a pallet fork to control rate.
escapement Parts of the movement which allow the power of the mainspring of a mechanical movement to "escape," converting the rotary motion of gear train into precise 'to-and-fro' motion.
FH Initials of the federation of the Swiss watch industry, the leading trade association.
form watch Any watch of unconventional shape.
frame Plates and pillars in movement.
frequency The vibrations per hour of mechanical watches (vph) or oscillations per second (Hz) of quartz ones. Most modern quartz watches have a frequency of 32,768 Hz.
guillochet Engine-turning – usually on the dial. A form of decoration.
hairspring or balance spring Spiral spring attached to arbor of balance to control oscillations.
Hertz Hz The number of oscillations per second of electronic watches.
horology The art and science of timekeeping.
incabloc A brand of shock absorber or protector designed to prevent damage to pinions or jewels.
jewels Used as bearings to reduce wear at points of greatest friction in movements. Usually 17–18 in mechanical watches. Once they were actually rubies, but are now synthetic.
karat A measure of the purity of precious metal alloys. Pure gold is 24 karat. 18 karat is more usual in top-quality watch cases and contains 18 parts of gold to six parts of other metals.
LCD Continuous liquid crystal display, of numerals in digital watch.
LED Light-emitting diode, the display of numerals in early digital quartz watches, operated by a button. Usually produces a red display.
lever or anchor escapement Part of a mechanical watch with a component shaped like an anchor, impulsing at each vibration to control the energy output of the mainspring. Derived from the escapement invented by Thomas Mudge in 1759.

ligne Used to indicate the size of a mechanical movement, measured over the plate beneath the dial. 1 ligne (‴) = 2.256mm (one twelfth of a "French inch").
limited-edition watch A watch produced in a strictly limited quantity and usually numbered to show its sequence in the series.
lug Parts of the case to which the bracelet or strap is attached. Also known as horns.
mainspring A flat spring coiled in the barrel which provides the power to drive the gear train of a mechanical watch.
mechanical watch Spring-driven watch with a regulatory system such as a pendulum or balance. May be hound-wound or automatic.
minute repeater A watch that sounds, or repeats hours, quarters, and sometimes minutes, at the press of a button or slide.
moon phase A display of phases of the moon in a window on the dial.
motion work Gear train for driving the hour hand from the minute wheel.
movement Complete mechanism of a watch.
oscillation The regular movement of a body, such as a balance wheel or pendulum, between two given points from one extreme to the other and back again.
pallet Small part of the escapement of a mechanical watch which meshes with the teeth of the escape wheel to transmit an impulse to the balance.
period The duration of an oscillation – one swing of the balance in each direction.
perpetual calendar Calendar mechanism which corrects itself for long and short months and leap years. Will continue until February 28, 2100.
pillars Posts between plates in the movement.
pinion Small toothed wheel.
pivot The fine ends of arbor which are mounted in jewels or plates.
power reserve (up and down) indicator Hand or window showing remaining hours of power before a mechanical watch will stop.
quartz Rock crystal (silicon dioxide) made to oscillate by electronic current. Maintains constant frequency according to its cut and mass. Synthetic material is sued in modern quarts watches.
radio controlled Quartz watches and clocks which receive a radio signal transmitted from a super-accurate cesium-atomic clock and use this signal to adjust themselves.
rattrapante A split-second function with flyback hand.
retrograde When referring to watches, it means hands that return swiftly to the starting point having traversed an arc completely.
roskopf watch Simplified mechanical watch invented in 1866 by G. F. Roskopf. The first cheap, rugged watch.
rotor Pivoted eccentric weight in an automatic watch which winds mainspring using energy from the wearer's movement. In Seiko's Kinetic watch, the eccentric rotor turns a mini-generator at speeds up to 100,000 rpm to generate electricity which is stored in a capacitor.
screw-down crown A threaded winding crown which screws tightly to the case to enhance water and dust resistance.
self-winding Automatic.
shock resistant A watch is judged to be shock-resistant if, when dropped onto a hard surface from height of 3 feet (1m), it does not stop, or if its daily rate does not afterwards change by more than 60 seconds per day.
skeleton watch One where most parts of the dial except the chapter ring have been removed to reveal the mechanism underneath. Often has a crystal case back as well.
solar-powered Watches with panels that capture light and convert it to electricity to power the quartz movement.
subsidiary dials Smaller dials, usually used to indicate elapsed hours, minutes, and seconds in a chronograph.
Swiss-made A term controlled by Swiss law which may only be used on watches meeting certain criteria: 50 percent of the parts must be Swiss-made; they must be assembled, finished, and inspected in Switzerland.
tachymetre (tachometer) Measuring system on the bezel or outer ring of the dial which can be used to calculate speed in miles or kilometers per hour.
tourbillon A mobile "cage" which holds the escapement of a mechanical watch movement and revolves, usually every 60 seconds, to overcome the effect of gravity on the running of a watch.
train Wheels and pinions which transmit power from the mainspring to the hands.
tritium Luminous paint for dials, numerals, or batons and hands; very slightly radioactive. Now being replaced by some manufacturers by other more effective and safer materials.
tuning fork Name given to the original electric watch which used a device similar in shape to a tuning fork. A transistor switch between two magnets. It harnesses the constant frequency of the tuning fork to regulate the watch.
vibration A half oscillation – i.e. a swing from one side to the other without returning to the original position. It is the measure of the frequency of mechanical watches (VpH).
water-resistant Watches which can withstand water pressure at depth of 1m (3.29 feet) for 30 minutes and thereafter for 90 seconds at 20m (65.6 feet). Most manufacturers avoid the term "waterproof," for which no international standard has been devised and which could be interpreted as having no limitation.
world time watch One which can display the current time in any time zone. Many show the time in two zones simultaneously.
yellow metal A term used only in Britain, where it is illegal under the hallmarking laws to describe a watch whose case or bracelet is bicolored, as "gold" and steel. Such watches are often referred to as "yellow metal" and steel.

INDEX

Page numbers in italics indicate an illustration only.

EBEL

Girard-Perregaux

BL

UNIVERSAL GENEVE

OMEGA

BAUME & MERCIER

Cartier Ltd

Christian Dior

DANIEL ROTI

CHRONOSWISS

Maurice Lacroix

CORUM

MDM
GENEVE

ULYSSE NARDI

JUNGHANS

BERTOLUCCI

CITIZEN

PERRELET